A New Owner's Guide to Australian Shepherds

JG-118

Overleaf: An Australian Shepherd adult and puppy.

Opposite page: Australian Shepherd photographed by Karen Taylor.

The author wishes to thank Stacy Kennedy for her editorial guidance.

The Publisher wishes to acknowledge the following owners of the dogs in this book: Jeannie Anderson, Lisa Cameron, Patricia Clark, Susan Clay, Karen Cox, Rick and Lydine Densin, Deborah Dodds, Jack Feir, Judith Frey, Brigdet Gallagher, Scott George, Heidi Gorschals, Ernest and Elaine Hartnagle, Joesph Hartnagle, Carol Ann Hartnagle-Madsen, Jeanne Joy Hartnagle-Taylor, Kathy Hauer, Mike Hofmeister, Lucinda Howard, Kelly Kemp, Michelle Kennedy, Linda LaFrance, Steven Levin, Roque Marquez, Steve and Carol Maslansky, Barbara McIntyre, Lorraine McLean, Brenda Olger, Caterina O'Sullivan, Claudia Pohmer, Heike Roeckel, Lois Rondeau, Judith Rose, Jack Ryen, Anita Simon-Laycock, Annie Souvill, Glenda Stephenson, Carol and Dan Thomsen, Thornapple Kennels, Roland Trub, Nola Ventura, Linda Wilson (Briarbrook), David and Vicky Whipp.

Photographers: Paulette Braun, Isabelle Francais, Joesph Hartnagle, Koler, Jillian Lisle, Marie Murphy, Robert Pearcy, Annie Souvill, Judith Strom, Trish Thornwell, Karen Taylor.

The author acknowledges the contribution of Judy Iby for the following chapters: Sport of Purebred Dogs, Traveling with Your Dog, Health Care, Dental Care, Identification and Finding the Lost Dog and Behavior and Canine Communication.

Distributed in the UNITED STATES to the Pet Trade by T.F.H. Publications, Inc., One T.F.H. Plaza, Neptune City, NJ 07753; distributed in the UNITED STATES to the Bookstore and Library Trade by National Book Network, Inc. 4720 Boston Way, Lanham MD 20706; in CANADA to the Pet Trade by H & L Pet Supplies Inc., 27 Kingston Crescent, Kitchener, Ontario N2B 2T6; Rolf C. Hagen Inc., 3225 Sartelon St. Laurent-Montreal Quebec H4R 1E8; in CANADA to the Book Trade by Vanwell Publishing Ltd., 1 Northrup Crescent, St. Catharines, Ontario L2M 6P5 ; in ENGLAND by T.F.H. Publications, PO Box 15, Waterlooville PO7 6BQ; in AUSTRALIA AND THE SOUTH PACIFIC by T.F.H. (Australia), Pty. Ltd., Box 149, Brookvale 2100 N.S.W., Australia; in NEW ZEALAND by Brooklands Aquarium Ltd. 5 McGiven Drive, New Plymouth, RD1 New Zealand; in Japan by T.F.H. Publications, Japan—Jiro Tsuda, 10-12-3 Ohjidai, Sakura, Chiba 285, Japan; in SOUTH AFRICA by Lopis (Pty) Ltd., P.O. Box 39127, Booysens, 2016, Johannesburg, South Africa. Published by T.F.H. Publications, Inc.

MANUFACTURED IN THE
UNITED STATES OF AMERICA
BY T.F.H. PUBLICATIONS, INC.

A New Owner's Guide to AUSTRALIAN SHEPHERDS

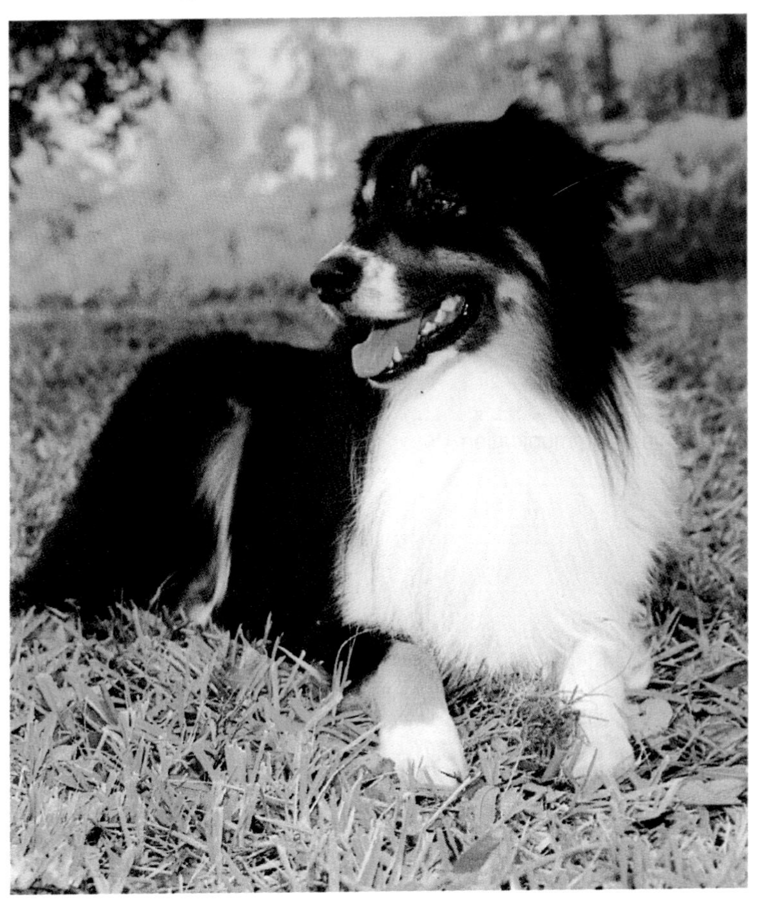

Joseph Hartnagle

Contents

1997 Edition

The Australian Shepherd has a long history as a rodeo dog.

Because the Aussie is so eager to please, he is one of the most trainable breeds in existence.

A well-cared for Aussie will be a healthy, loving companion for many years.

The Australian Shepherd is a high-energy dog that loves physical activity.

The Aussie is a hardy working breed, known for his herding abilities.

HISTORY of the Australian Shepherd

The origin of The Australian Shepherd is not definitely known. Despite their name, Australian Shepherds are not from Australia. There has even been speculation that they might be a remnant of the lost continent of Atlantis. According to early owners and breeders, Aussies were introduced to Australia from the Basque region in the Pyrenees Mountains between Spain and France. For lack of enough employment in their own land, the Basques migrated to other countries, taking their dogs with them. These colorful little dogs acquired their name as they arrived in the United States with the boatloads of Australian sheep and their Basque sheepherders. This took place in the late 1800s and early 1900s as the American wool market was blossoming.

The Australian Shepherd is intelligent and extremely willing to please, allowing him to excel in any task he undertakes. Owner, Barbara McIntyre.

Stockmen were impressed with the abilities of these capable dogs, which were used for herding cattle as much as sheep. Their popularity began to rise throughout the western United States. It wasn't until the 1950s and '60s, when Jay Sisler, a rodeo contestant and rancher from Idaho, teamed up with Shorty, Stubby and Queenie that the Australian Shepherd gained national attention. Jay and his

Australian Shepherds have long been an integral part of ranching in the western United States, becoming indispensable to the cattlemen whose livelihood depends on them.

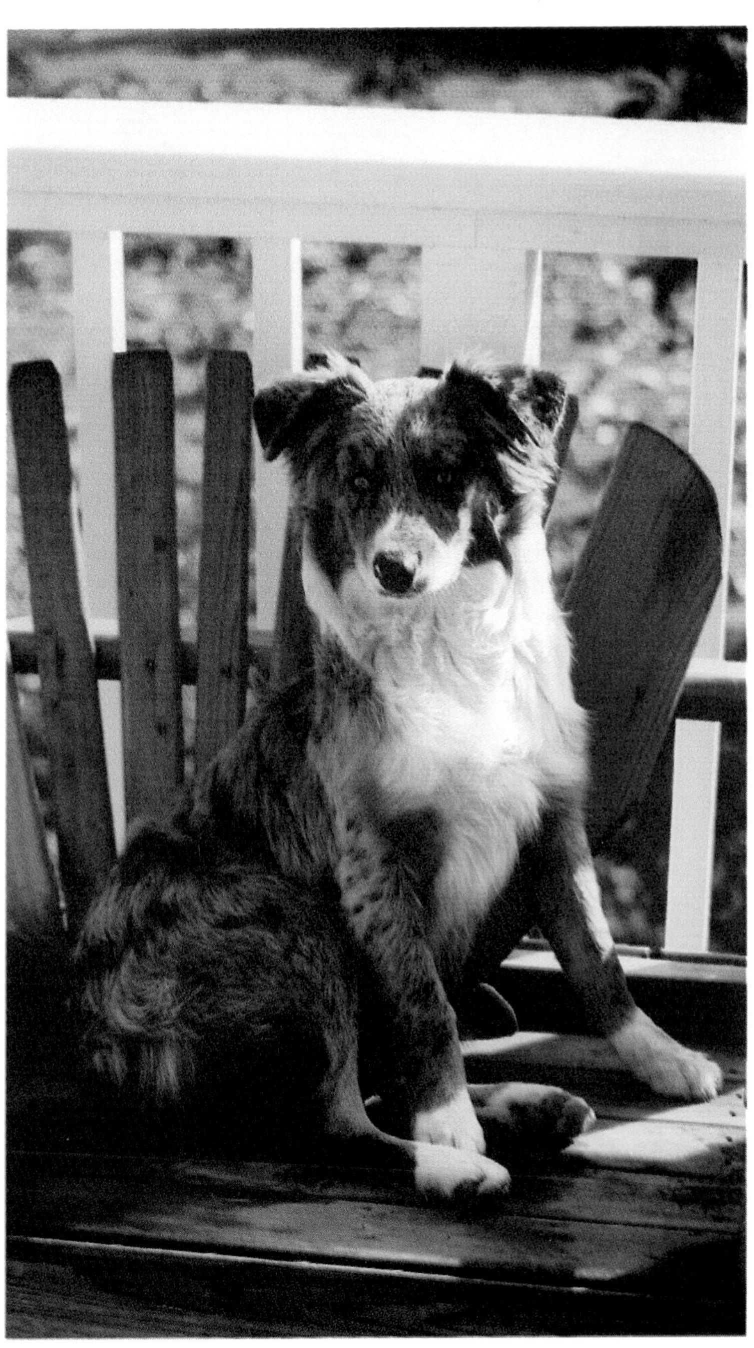

Aussies delighted rodeo audiences throughout the United States and Canada with an array of tricks that have yet to be equaled even today. In fact, so unique and delightful were these dogs that Walt Disney Studios produced two movies featuring them: *Stub, The World's Greatest Cowdog*, and *Run, Appaloosa, Run.*

Juanita Ely, the dean of old-time Australian Shepherd breeders, acquired her first Aussie during the 1920s when she imported a boatload of sheep from Australia. When the sheep arrived in the United States they were accompanied by a Basque sheepherder and a little blue dog.

Mrs. Ely later bought a female from Jay Sisler, Ely's Blue, a full sister to Sisler's Queenie, the famous trick dog. Ely's Blue produced Hartnagle's Badger and Hartnagle's Goody (who later became known as Blue Shadow, an ancestor of both the well-known Wood and Flintridge bloodlines).

The breed continued to grow and breed true to type as it had for generations. Foundation bloodlines were established and the modern Australian Shepherd developed from there. Among the most influential sires of the modern Australian Shepherd include Sisler's Shorty, Wood's Jay, George's Red Rustler, Wildhagen's Dutchman and Las Rocosa Shiloh. Wildhagen's Thistle and Hartnagle's Fritzie Taylor were responsible for producing a number of outstanding sires and dams who, in turn, laid the foundation for many modern bloodlines recognized in the Australian Shepherd Club of America Hall of Fame and Record of Merit.

During the early years, most Aussie activity took place in

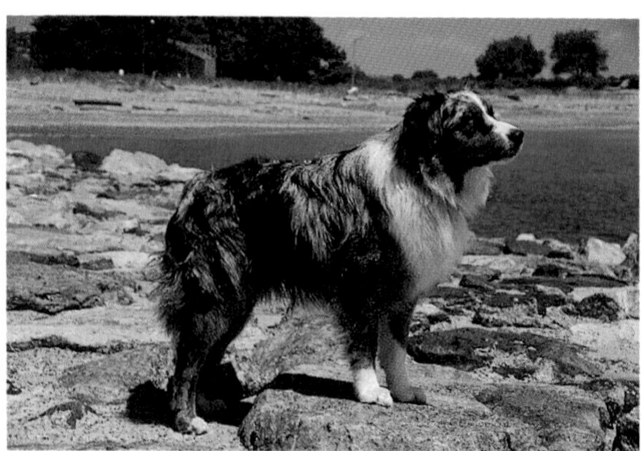

Early imports of the Australian Shepherd bred true to type, giving us the breed we know today.

Arizona, California, Colorado and the Pacific Northwest. Early promoters and breeders included Jay Sisler, Juanita Ely, the Hartnagles, Don Brezeale, the Thorntons, Vicky Mistretta, Weldon Heard and Fletcher Wood.

These Aussie puppies are as at home in the sun as their Arizona-bred ancestors.

As the breed continued to win the devoted following of many fanciers, Aussie clubs were formed. A network of correspondence provided a small but growing membership throughout the United States. The Australian Shepherd Club of America (ASCA) was founded in Tucson, Arizona, in June 1957. By special arrangement, The International English Shepherd Registry (known as The National Stock Dog Registry) became the official registry of the Australian

The Australian Shepherd has come a long way, but still does dual duty as a working dog and a beloved household pet. Ch. Just Jake of Las Rocosa with Jason Renna.

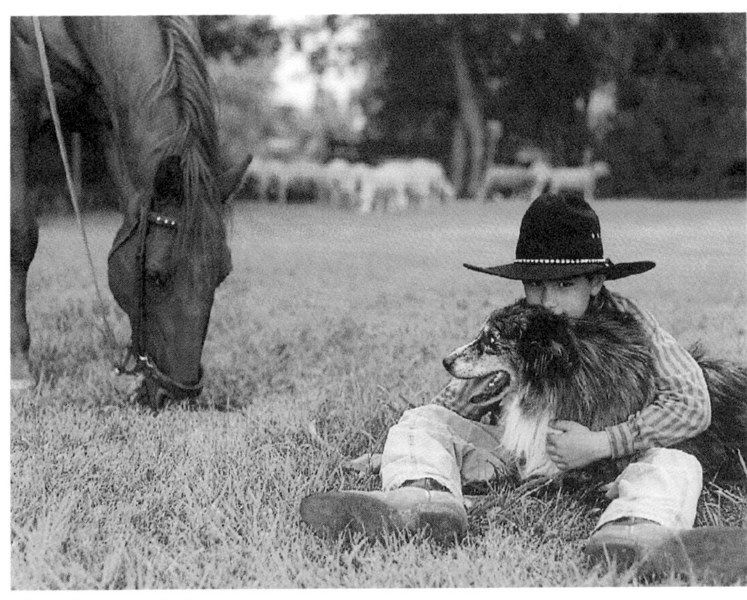

Shepherd. In 1971, ASCA's registry became functional. The club developed programs to encourage activity and further promote the Australian Shepherd breed. A formal show program was created for members so their dogs could gain conformation championships, obedience titles and tracking degrees.

A stock dog program was initiated to help preserve the inherited herding instincts of these agile, athletic, working dogs. Certification for stock dog titles could be earned for qualifying work at sanctioned trials.

In 1991, Aussies were officially recognized by the Canadian Kennel Club and by the American Kennel Club. Currently, there are five associations for registering and competing with Aussies: ASCA (Australian Shepherd Club of America), AKC (American Kennel Club), CKC (Canadian Kennel Club), UKC (United Kennel Club) and NSDR (National Stock Dog Registry).

In ASCA, the original parent club for Australian Shepherds, Aussies can earn titles in herding (stockdog), agility, conformation, obedience and tracking programs. For more information contact: ASCA, 6091 E. State Hwy 21, Bryan, Texas 77808-9652, or call 1-800-892-ASCA.

Aussie breeders strive to preserve the breed's herding instincts but also show and compete in other activities. Ch. Herry, owned by Heidi Gorchals.

As his flock quietly grazes, the noble Aussie stands guard. This is Hall of Fame Sire WTCh. Las Rocosa Bonny Kyle bred by Jeanne Joy Hartnagle-Taylor.

AKC also offers herding, agility, conformation, obedience and tracking programs. Rules and regulations can be obtained by writing to AKC, 51 Madison Ave, New York, NY, 10010, or call 919-233-9767.

In Canada, Aussies are eligible to compete in conformation, obedience, junior showmanship, and tracking programs. Contact CKC by writing to them at Commerce Park, 89 Skyway Avenue, Suite 100, Etobicoke, Ontario, Canada M9W 6R4, or call 416-675-5511. The UKC also offers performance events for Aussies. Contact the UKC at 100 East Kilgore Road, Kalamazoo, MI 49001-5598, or call 616- 343-9020.

The NSDR offers a working program and also registers miniature Aussies. Their address is NSDR, 3597 CO RD 75, PO Box 402, Butler, IN 46271.

As their popularity continues to grow, Australian Shepherds are rapidly gaining recognition with fanciers throughout Europe, Japan, Mexico and Puerto Rico.

CHARACTERISTICS of the Australian Shepherd

Aussies are superb guardians, loyal companions and energetic playmates. Aussies are agile, weather-resistant and hardy. All of these traits stem from hundreds of years working outdoors in all weather as dependable herders and guardians of livestock in often unfriendly terrains. Aussies are working dogs first and foremost.

Both AKC and ASCA breed standards describe Aussies as intelligent, naturally reserved, versatile, active and easily trained, with strong herding and guarding instincts. Emphasis is placed on the versatility and working aspects of the breed, but peculiarities not evident in the show (conformation) ring are not included.

After hundreds of years of working outdoors, the Aussie is a hardy, resilient dog that quickly adapts to any kind of weather. Owners, Mike Hofmeister and Heike Roeckel.

Aussies are quick to learn and eager to please. Although Aussies are biddable, they are not robots that can be trained to obey without thinking. They are among the highly intelligent, elite group of herding breeds that have the uncanny ability to think with the initiative to figure things out on their own. If the master tells his Aussie to come home, but is unaware that a newborn lamb or injured ewe may be hidden in a ravine or behind some brush, the Aussie's inherited character is either to bring in the stray or stay with it and protect it from harm.

Aussies are adoring and affectionate with family members, but suspicious and watchful of strangers. This is not to imply

Aussies are superb guardians and ideal family dogs. They are natural "baby-sitters" and great playmates for any child.

they are shy or timid. Aussies are territorial; they have a strong sense of boundaries and they protect their turf from intruders.

Aussies are not going to joyfully welcome everyone who walks in the door unannounced and give them a guided tour of the house, and they shouldn't, considering their heritage as guardians. If your home is an open house to the neighborhood with non-stop kids running in and out and different people coming and going, you need to be prepared to make proper introductions.

Aussies are high-energy dogs and not well suited to a couch-potato lifestyle. They are not good companions for people who hate to exercise or walk in inclement weather. Nor are they suited to busy households with little time to train or play with them. Aussies want to interact with their owners and sometimes will follow them from room to room just for their companionship.

Because the Aussie is so eager to please, he is one of the most trainable breeds in existence. This is Loura Fourre with Ch. Las Rocosa Tomichi Pilgrim, CDX.

Due to their highly adaptable nature and willingness to please, Aussies are extraordinarily versatile and able to perform in many different functions. What they don't do by instinct they can be taught with a minimum of training. Aussies do extremely well in obedience, agility trials, flyball and Frisbee® competitions. Aussies excel in the service of man in a wide variety of roles, be it farm and ranch work, bomb and drug detection or search and rescue work. And that by no means covers the talents of this amazing breed. Aussies are happiest when pleasing their masters.

Aussies are devoted family dogs and fond of children when reared with them. They will protect their charges from harm, often placing themselves between the child and a dangerous situation, then gently urge the child away. Aussies have been known to even grasp a child's hand or garment and actually tug the child toward safety.

One such dog, a soulful, brown-eyed Aussie named Pepper, rescued her young friend from a rattlesnake. The two-year-old girl was playing in her grandmother's backyard when all of a sudden she began screaming in fright. When the grandmother ran to the back porch she heard the rattling and saw the snake wrapped around the little girl's leg. Meanwhile, the Aussie exploded. She lunged at the three-foot rattler, bit into it near the head and tore it from the child's leg. The child was bitten once in the heel, and Pepper received six bites to the top of the head. The child was rushed to the hospital immediately for treatment. The family was told by the doctor that the child was going to be fine, but if it had been five minutes later the child would probably have been in a coma. As luck would have it, the snake bit into a bony area of Pepper's head where the poison didn't travel and the little Aussie was okay, too.

Whether they are sheep, cattle or man, all his charges are well protected under the watchful eye of the Australian Shepherd.

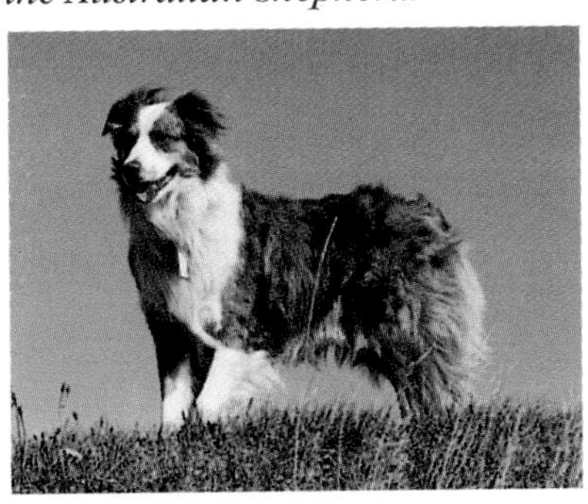

Aussies exhibit undying loyalty to their owners. There are numerous tales of these dogs keeping vigil over a gravely ill or dead master until help arrived, guarding the body. As one owner related, "I had an accident with my horse. I was dragging a calf out of a gully with my rope, and the horse came over backwards and crushed me, separating my pelvis and fracturing my back. Ordinarily, my dog Kentucky Badger is ebullient, and if you lay on the ground he is all over you wanting to play. In this instance he immediately understood that I was hurt. He wormed and snuffled his way under my head while I was lying on the ground waiting for the pickup to come and carry me back to the house. The same situation was repeated in the truck. When the ambulance men loaded me on the stretcher he nipped at one of them just to remind them that they best treat me gently.

"Of course, big events like that one stick out in my memory, but more important over the long haul is the day-to-day job that he does with me taking care of the cattle on the farm. I manage 2,300 acres here, and we have large pastures with poor fencing. I don't know how my wife and I could handle the cattle without him. I wouldn't try. He helps us put the horses to bed and is the finest watchdog I've ever seen. I can tell from his bark whether the car coming up the lane is my wife returning from town or a stranger, or if his barking means that one of the horses is out, or if a calf or cow is loose. All the scientists in the world are welcome to believe that dogs can't smile, but I know that my Kentucky Badger can."

The Australian Shepherd was first brought to national attention through the rodeo shows of the '50s and '60s. This is Dally, with rodeo clown Kevin "Bunky" Hall.

"Cold, heat, rain, or snow, it doesn't matter to him as long as he knows that there is a job to be done. I know that he wouldn't like it, and he would let me know he didn't, but if I had to hike through hell he'd be right there with me all the way."

Aussies have an intense herding instinct and the uncanny ability to sense weather changes and severe storms. One gentle female, Topaz, brought 50 head of cattle off the range into the home corral, arriving within minutes of a raging blizzard that paralyzed the entire area before her master had realized the near predicament upon them. Another Aussie, sensing disaster, drove a small ranch herd out of a dry wash onto higher ground shortly before a flash flood hit that would have destroyed the entire herd. In this instance the owner was away from his ranch on that day.

One owner from Tennessee summed it up when she said, "Our Aussie does everything with a certain flair. She finished her championship with three major wins and her obedience titles with High in Trial awards. She works stock, catches Frisbees®, performs rodeo tricks (or did in her younger days) and has produced Best of Breed winners. But most of all, we think she is outstanding because she has returned love and

devotion a thousand fold. Several years ago, while on a camping trip, she saved a seven-year-old child from drowning in a river."

Australian Shepherds are clever workers. Their natural herding ability is exhibited by the tendency to round up even people, and they will try to do this without any special training. When left unsupervised or when bored, this tendency can lead to the annoying and dangerous activity of chasing cars, bicycles or the neighbor's cat.

Aussies are alert watchdogs and will naturally protect family members, the family car, house and yard, a litter of puppies or a child. If left chained up or confined in a small enclosure without adequate daily exercise, attention and training, Aussies can develop behavioral problems and uncharacteristic aggression.

Aussies thrive on human companionship. Unless the owners have the time or are willing to make time to spend with a dog every day, then they are too busy to own an Aussie. While some Aussies are able to adapt to the stress and confinement of city living, the majority of Aussies (both show and working bloodlines) are energetic and need plenty of regular (daily) outdoor exercise and training. Australian Shepherds are a more practical choice for an active owner or family in the suburbs or the country.

THE WORKING AUSTRALIAN SHEPHERD

Ranching, particularly in the western United States, would have been almost impossible without the willing obedience and instincts of the Australian Shepherd. For hundreds of years, herding dogs have been used in many ways to man's

Australian Shepherds thrive on human companionship. The love you give to your Aussie will be returned with affection and undying loyalty.

advantage. In handling a herd of cattle or flock of sheep out on the range, a good working dog more than equals the work of three men on horseback.

The Aussie's natural herding instincts are effective on all kinds of livestock, including goats.

Aussies are authoritative, assertive workers. They are naturally a close-working breed, ideal for farm or ranch work. Their natural instinct is to control and herd livestock. Even as puppies this instinct is evident when you see your puppy stalking birds in the yard, ducks on a pond or the sheep in a field. In fact, the herding instinct is so strong in some individuals that without an appropriate outlet they will try to round up anything that moves–including unyielding and dangerous automobiles.

The herding instinct is an adaptation of the ancient hunting drives of wolves, their remote ancestors. These instincts were modified for human

The Australian Shepherd is happiest with plenty of outdoor activities and exercise. This is Poco and Tyler Taylor.

needs. Wolves hunt in packs, with the faster members outrunning the prey to turn them back to the slower members, who get into position to make the kill and prevent the prey from getting away. That killing instinct has long since been bred out, resulting in the modern herding instincts of the working Australian Shepherd.

Aussies who constantly run to the head of livestock and try to stop them would have been the faster members of the pack, while the individuals who follow behind the livestock would have been the slower members. The head dogs are often referred to as fetching or gathering dogs because they round up and try to take the stock to their trainer. The individuals who follow from behind are called driving dogs. Common among the driving dogs is the instinct to grip the heels of a stubborn straggler, called heeling. In puppies, this instinct is displayed during play when they nip the heels of their littermates or the pants leg of their master. The fetching and gathering dogs frequently will grip the nose of a challenging animal when necessary to assert authority.

In training the Aussie for work on livestock, the trainer enhances these natural instincts by providing opportunities and guidance for the young Aussie to learn how to think and control the stock in a manageable situation–such as a round pen (50 to 60 feet across)–during the first lessons. In this area, the trainer can help the Aussie learn how to balance the livestock by herding by guiding him to move not too close or too wide from his stock.

The basis for training the Aussie for trial work is no different than training it for any other type of work with livestock. For competition, however, it is necessary to develop more finesse and polish than for everyday work. Aussie trials have steadily increased in popularity since they were introduced in 1973. While it is nearly impossible to hold trials that are not in some degree artificial, they do provide competitors and spectators alike with similar conditions to test the cleverness of a skilled dog and handler.

Stock dogs are used in many different situations, some of that are dissimilar to trial work. A good farm or ranch Aussie should be able to hold his own in the trial arena. On the other hand, an Aussie used to handling stock in adverse circumstances may not excel in the trial arena, although still an excellent stock dog. By the same token, you can have a good trial dog that has been trained for precise direction from his handler that, when placed in a situation where he has to think on his own, becomes lost and ineffective.

Trials for the Australian Shepherd test each dog's ability to maneuver sheep, goats, cattle and/or ducks through a series of obstacles. Secondly, they determine how well dog and master work as a team. Different courses are usually offered at each trial. Each Aussie has the same allotted time in which to complete the assigned work. While it is possible for two dogs to complete their work in the same amount of time, one may garner more points for the quality of work accomplished while on the course. However, it is far more desirable for a dog who is in balance and control of his stock to miss getting the total number of animals through an obstacle than to gallop around and around and by chance have them run through all the obstacles.

Australian Shepherd trials test the breed's ability to control a herd and work with their masters. Cassie, owned by Jack Ryen, is herding sheep.

STANDARD for the Australian Shepherd

A standard is a blueprint for a breed. The breed standard is the "ideal" toward which breeders gear their breeding programs. The standard for the Aussie is a written description of an ideal, fully mature Australian Shepherd. All terminology used in the breed standard is common to breeders and judges in the dog fancy. It was written to preserve correct form. Each anatomical feature was developed for a specific purpose. The Aussie's inherent duties dictated his type.

The breed standard is also a guide by which dog show judges evaluate Aussies in a conformation show.

The Australian Shepherd is an athletic, well balanced dog of medium build. This is Las Rocosa Henery, CDX, owned by Susan Clay.

The American Kennel Club uses the AKC breed standard for Aussies, while the Australian Shepherd Club of America, The Canadian Kennel Club and The United Kennel Club use the ASCA standard. The AKC standard is printed here in its entirety, with differences in the ASCA standard listed below each section, and commentary by the author in italics.

Official AKC Standard for the Australian Shepherd

General Appearance—The Australian Shepherd is an intelligent working dog of strong herding and guarding instincts. He is a loyal companion and has the stamina to work all day. He is well balanced, slightly longer than tall, of medium size and bone, with coloring that offers variety and individuality. He is attentive and animated, lithe and agile, solid and muscular, without cloddiness. He has a coat of moderate length and coarseness. He has a docked or natural bobbed tail.

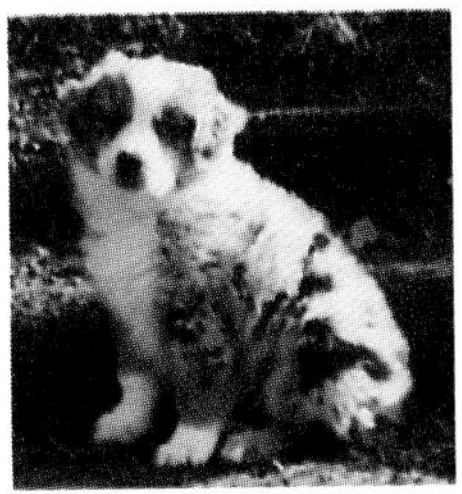

The Australian Shepherd puppy is a miniature version of the adult. Owner, Nola Ventura.

The section on general appearance is intended as a visual description of the first impression one has of an Aussie. It includes only the features that are apparent at some distance and distinguish the Aussie from all other breeds of dogs. In this section as well as throughout the standard, emphasis is placed on the balance and a sense of moderation indicative of the breed. Australian Shepherds should be moderate in every aspect of their appearance. Coat is of moderate length, neither long or short.

Size, Proportion, Substance—*Size*—The preferred height for males is 20 to 23 inches, females 18 to 21 inches. Quality is not to be sacrificed in favor of size. *Proportion*—Measuring from the breastbone to rear of thigh and from top of the withers to the ground, the Australian Shepherd is slightly longer than tall. *Substance*—Solidly built with moderate bone. Structure in the male reflects masculinity without coarseness. Bitches appear feminine without being slight of bone.

The Aussie is medium sized with bone to match, neither heavy nor course or small boned or refined. His appearance reflects beauty and utilitarian function.

The length of his head from the tip of his nose to the upper back tip of the skull to the withers is equidistant. To further contribute to the total picture of balance, the length of the upper arm approximates the length of the shoulder blade and the elbow is of equal distance from the ground to the withers.

When first viewing the breed, you should not have to measure each anatomical feature, as the balance and moderation should be apparent in the initial impression. The ideal Aussie should not have any glaring faults or features. The Aussie's form truly follows and reflects its intended function. The body is slightly longer than tall to lend to agility and enable him to turn on a dime should he need to get away from hooves and horns.

The docked or natural bobbed tail further identifies the breed from a distance.

Head—The *Head* is clean-cut, strong and dry. Overall size should be in proportion to the body. The muzzle is equal in length or slightly shorter than the back skull. Viewed from the side the topline of the back skull and muzzle form parallel planes, divided by a moderate, well-defined stop. The muzzle tapers little from base to nose and is rounded at the tip. *Expression*—Showing attentiveness and intelligence, alert and eager. Gaze should be keen but friendly. *Eyes* are brown, blue, amber or any variation or combination thereof, including flecks and marbling. Almond-shaped, not protruding nor sunken. The blue merles and blacks have black pigmentation on eye rims. The red merles and reds have liver (brown) pigmentation on eye rims. *Ears* are triangular, of moderate size and leather, set high on the head. At full attention they break forward and over, or to the side as a rose ear. Prick ears and hanging ears are *severe faults*. *Skull*—Top flat to slightly domed. It may show a slight occipital protuberance. Length and width are equal. Moderate well-defined stop.

An Aussie's eyes can be brown, amber, blue, or any variation of the three. This puppy's clear blue eyes are a striking example.

An Australian Shepherd's expression should show his keen intelligence, alertness and friendly demeanor. This is Ch. Gun River She's So Fine, owned by Brenda Olger.

Muzzle tapers little from base to nose and is rounded at the tip. *Nose*–Blue merles and blacks have black pigmentation on the nose (and lips). Red merles and reds have liver pigmentation on the nose (and lips). On the merles it is permissible to have small pink spots; however, they should not exceed 25 percent of the nose on dogs over 1 year of age, which is a *serious fault*. *Teeth*–A full complement of strong white teeth should meet in a scissors bite or may meet in a level bite. *Disqualifications*–Undershot. Overshot greater than one-eighth of an inch. Loss of contact caused by short center incisors in an otherwise correct bite shall not be judged undershot. Teeth broken or missing by accident shall not be penalized.

ASCA: Head–"...its length and width each equal to the length of the muzzle....The muzzle tapers slightly to a rounded tip."

ASCA: Expression–"Very expressive, showing attentiveness and intelligence. Clear, almond-shaped and of moderate size, set a little obliquely, neither prominent nor sunken, with pupils dark, well-defined and perfectly positioned."

ASCA: Ears–"The ears, at full attention, break slightly forward and over from one-quarter to one-half above the base. Prick ears and hound-type ears are severe faults."

ASCA: Teeth–"A full complement of strong white teeth should meet in a scissors bite. An even bite is a fault. Disqualifications: Undershot bites; overshot bites exceeding $^1/_8$ inches."

ASCA: Nose–"Butterfly nose should not be faulted under one year of age."

The shape of the Australian Shepherd's head is determined by the bones below the eyes (zygomatic arch), ridge on the top of the skull (sagittal crest) and the position of the bottom jaw.

The structure of the skull should be in balance to and compliment the overall appearance described under "General Appearance." The length and width of the topskull equal the length of the muzzle, which tapers from the tip of the nose and follows the underline of the jaw to the base.

The flat to slightly rounded or domed ridge on the topskull allows for protection from a blow on the head–such as can occur when working cattle–the domed ridge allows for the adequate attachment of muscles, which are used for biting. The scissors bite, as described under "Teeth," influences the shape of the muzzle to taper slightly.

Clean-cut and dry describe a head that is free from loose or hanging skin. The skin is tight and muscled immediately below the surface.

The section on teeth describes the "bite," which is the position of the top jaw in relation to the bottom jaw. In the scissors bite, which is ideal for the breed, the top jaw and teeth slightly overlap the bottom ones. The level or even bite acquired its name because the top and bottom jaw meet evenly. In the undershot bite, the bottom jaw protrudes beyond the upper jaw, and in the overshot bite, the top jaw protrudes beyond the bottom jaw. Due to the unsound nature of overshot and undershot bites, this serious fault results in disqualification from the conformation show ring and should not be used for breeding. A full complement of teeth means that each adult Aussie has 42 teeth made of four different types of teeth: 12 incisors, 4 canine teeth, 16 premolars and 10 molars.

The correct shape and slightly oblique position of the eyes dictates the almond shape, which lends a fairly wide field of vision and protection for the eyes. There is no preference for any one eye color over another.

The eye color can be in any combination or variation of blue, brown and/or amber, including flecks of another color or marbling of the iris. Even when the eyes are marbled, the pupil is dark and well-defined.

The Australian Shepherd has retained his acute sense of hearing because he has the ability to erect his ears to catch sound waves. Aussies can move their ears forward and backward, or independently of one another to locate and follow sound.

An example of the Aussie's clean-cut, well proportioned head and almond-shaped eyes, definitive of the breed. This is Las Rocosa Sugar Candy, owned by Annie Souvill.

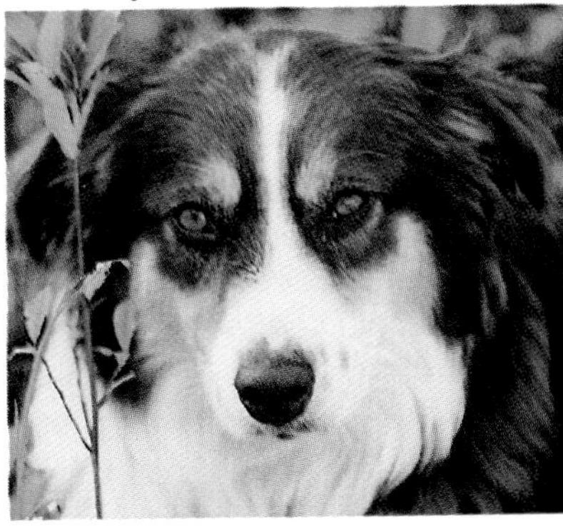

The shape of the skull, the tightness of the skin and the muscles beneath the skin's surface contribute to the Aussie's ear-set and type.

The same bones that influence the shape of the skull and eyes also affect the placement of the ears. The moderate length of ear leather balances the total head. The length of the ear can be measured easily by guiding the tip of the ear to the inside corner of the eye. As long as the ears are of moderate size, triangular-shaped and set high on the head, they are allowed to vary as to where they break over. When the Aussie's ears are erect they lend to an alert, keen expression. Although prick ears are faulted, they do exist in every foundation bloodline of Australian Shepherds and do not affect the breed's soundness or detract from the Aussie's ability as a working dog or companion.

Pigmentation (black- or liver-colored) on the nose leather is necessary to protect the nose from sun exposure. The dudley nose (one without pigmentation) constitutes a serious fault because it leaves the nose vulnerable to sunburn.

Pink spots on the nose that are surrounded by pigmentation will usually fill in with age, due to the breed's tendency for the coat color to become darker with age.

Neck, Topline, Body—*Neck* is strong, of moderate length, slightly arched at the crest, fitting well into the shoulders. *Topline*—Back is straight and strong, level and firm from withers to hip joints. The croup is moderately sloped. *Chest* is not broad but is deep with the lowest point reaching the elbow. The ribs are well sprung and long, neither barrel-chested nor slab-sided. The underline shows a moderate tuck-up. *Tail* is straight, docked or naturally bobbed, not to exceed four inches in length.

The Aussie's body is essentially designed for agility and stamina. Slightly longer than tall, it lends itself to a low center of gravity necessary for total maneuverability. The neck should be set well into the shoulders to yield correct balance and contribute to flexibility and endurance.

Well-sprung ribs protect the lungs, heart and other organs. The loin must be strong and broad enough to join the forequarters to the hindquarters. Many Aussies are born with naturally bobbed tails. Aussies born with tails are docked shortly after birth. Natural bobbed or docked, the length is not to exceed four inches at maturity. The practice of docking stems back to the days when a bobbed tail

Hall of Fame Sire Ch. Fieldmaster Three Ring Circus shows the straight strong back, deep chest and naturally bobbed tail required by the breed.

identified working dogs, thus exempting their owners from taxes.

Forequarters—*Shoulders*—Shoulder blades are long, flat, fairly close set at the withers and well laid back. The upper arm, which should be relatively the same length as the shoulder blade, attaches at an approximate right angle to the shoulder line with forelegs dropping straight, perpendicular to the ground. *Legs* straight and strong. Bone is strong, oval rather than round. *Pastern* is medium length and very slightly sloped. Front dewclaws may be removed. *Feet* are oval, compact with close-knit, well arched toes. Pads are thick and resilient.

The shoulders and legs of the Australian Shepherd must be strong in order to withstand shock while running and turning.

ASCA: Forequarters—"Pasterns are short, thick and strong, but still flexible showing a slight angle when viewed from the side."

The forequarters must support over half of the entire body weight and be flexible and strong enough to withstand shock while running and turning. The bone lengths and relative angles allows the Aussie quick bursts of speed to be able to outrun livestock and the stamina to travel all day over rough terrain. The feet must be strong and compact in order to effectively support the body and absorb initial shock. The strong yet flexible pasterns further contribute to the shock-absorbing qualities of the forequarters.

Hindquarters—The width of the hindquarters is equal to the width of the forequarters at the shoulders. The angulation of the pelvis and upper thigh corresponds to the angulation of the shoulder blade and upper arm, forming an approximate right angle. *Stifles* are clearly defined, hock joints moderately bent. The *hocks* are short, perpendicular to the ground and parallel to each other when viewed from the rear. Rear dewclaws must be removed. *Feet* are oval, compact with close-knit, well arched toes. Pads are thick and resilient.

The width of the hindquarters equals the width of the forequarters. The angles of the rear assembly must be compatible with the angles of the front assembly. While the hindquarters support less weight, they must work in synchronization with the front as they propel the Aussie forward effortlessly and efficiently.

Coat—Hair is of medium texture, straight to wavy, weather resistant and of medium length. The undercoat varies in quantity with variations in climate. Hair is short and smooth on the head, ears, front of forelegs and below the hocks. Backs of forelegs and britches are moderately feathered. There is a moderate mane and frill, more pronounced in dogs than in bitches. Non-typical coats are *severe faults*.

ASCA: Coat—"Of medium texture, straight to slightly wavy."

The Aussie's double coat (a longer outer coat with shorter underlayer) offers two important functions. The outer layer protects the skin from sunburn, while the underlayer acts as the insulator and traps the air between the Aussie's skin and the outside elements to protect it from the cold. Consequently, it will vary with climatic conditions.

The outer coat should be straight to slightly wavy, not curly. One of the appealing features to Aussie fanciers is their wide array of colors. The attractive blue, red or black color patterns may be complimented with or without white and/or tan (copper) trim.

Color—Blue merle, black, red merle, red—all with or without white markings and/or tan (copper) points, with no order of preference. The hairline of a white collar does not exceed the point of the withers at the skin. White is acceptable on the neck (either in part or as a full collar), chest, legs, muzzle underparts, blaze on head and white extension from underpart up to four inches, measuring from a horizontal line at the elbow. White on the head should not predominate, and the eyes must be fully surrounded by color and pigment. Merles characteristically become darker with increasing age. *Disqualifications*—White body splashes, which means white on body between withers and tail, on sides between elbows and back of hindquarters in all colors.

ASCA: Color—"On all colors the areas surrounding the ears and eyes must be fully surrounded by color and pigment."

The blue or red color when expressed in the merle patterns can be flecked, speckled, mottled, marbled, splotched with large patches throughout the coat or in any combination of the above. Black Aussies should be coal black with corresponding eye rims, lips and nose leather. The blue merles should also have black skin pigmentation, but instead of solid black, the merling will combine jet-black hair with white hair to create the various merle patterns, which appear as deep as steel blue, as bright as silver blue or as light as powder blue.

Unlike the blues and blacks, the red and red-merle Aussies must have liver skin pigmentation. The reddish-brown color can be as dark as liver, or burgundy to rust or chestnut colored. All colors must be clear and rich regardless of the hue.

Red and red merle Aussies can have blue, brown and/or amber colored eyes in any color combination or pattern with flecks or marbling of another color. Blue and black Aussies can have either blue or brown eyes in any combination.

The attractive merle color patterns are associated with the dominant state of the homozygous merle gene that can

An Aussie's coat can come in a variety of colors and markings, giving each dog his own individual appearance. This is a black tri-colored mom and her red merle puppy.

potentate deafness and/or blindness. This gene manifests itself when two merle Aussies (of either color) are mated together. When the puppies are born they appear to be white or predominately white.

Gait—The Australian Shepherd has a smooth, free and easy gait. He exhibits great agility of movement with a well-balanced, ground-covering stride. Fore and hind legs move straight and parallel with the center line of the body. As speed increases, the feet (front and rear) converge toward the center line of gravity of the dog while the back remains firm and level. The Australian Shepherd must be agile and able to change direction or alter gait instantly.

The Aussie must be light on his feet and at any given moment be able to change the speeds of his gait. He must be able to go from a walk where three feet are touching the ground, to a gallop, when only one foot is in contact with the ground and supporting the entire weight. When galloping there may be brief moments when the Aussie is airborne. Many times throughout a working day the Aussie will trot with only two feet (always the diagonally opposite ones) on the ground at any one time. The coordination between the front assembly and the hindguarters must be synchronized. This interplay between the hindquarters is most easily judged from the trot. When the forequarters and the hindquarters are correctly synchronized, a split second after the front paw is lifted off the ground, the hind paw will touch and fill its place. When the Aussie is moving in a trot away from the viewer, the legs will form a "V" shape.

The Australian Shepherd has a smooth, free and easy gait and is able to stop and start, or change directions, easily.

The most important feature of the Aussie's gait is that all components work together to contribute to his athletic ability enabling him to alter direction or gait instantly.

Temperament—The Australian Shepherd is an intelligent,

Although he may be wary of strangers at first, an Aussie should ultimately possess a good-natured, even temperament. Owner, Jeannie Anderson.

active dog with an even disposition; he is good-natured, seldom quarrelsome. He may be somewhat reserved in initial meetings. *Faults*—Any display of shyness, fear or aggression is to be severely penalized.

ASCA: Character—"He is reserved with strangers but does not exhibit shyness."

Disqualifications—Undershot. Overshot greater than one-eighth of an inch. White body splashes, which means white on body between withers and tail, on sides between elbows and back of hindquarters in all colors.

ASCA: Disqualifications—"Other than recognized colors. White body splashes. Dudley nose. Undershot bites; overshot bites exceeding one-eighth inches. Monorchidism and cryptorchidism."

SELECTING an Australian Shepherd

Aussies come in such an interesting and beautiful array of coat colors that sometimes buyers can become clouded in their decision when choosing the individual puppy best suited to them. When it comes to making an Aussie a new family member, the results of a hasty decision have far greater consequences than when purchasing an inanimate object.

Choosing the perfect puppy takes tremendous thought and consideration. This dog will be a part of the family for many years to come. While the personality of the puppy is the most important feature for a compatible relationship, a few other factors should be evaluated as well.

The Aussie's coat is easy to care for, but does shed and requires brushing. If you are opposed to occasional stray hairs on your black pants or new wool suit, look elsewhere.

This litter of Australian Shepherd puppies seems irresistible, but educate yourself about the responsibilities of owning a puppy before bringing one home.

Your Aussie puppy will have a great start in life if his mother and father are healthy and well adjusted. If possible, meet the puppy's parents before taking him home.

Can't decide between a male or female? Females come into heat twice a year, which requires special care to prevent unwanted puppies and the nuisance of attracting unwanted males. They also shed more after each heat cycle. Spaying a female will prevent both these problems. Males, on the other hand, can stray to find a female in heat. However, leg lifting and roaming are not problems in neutered males or those that are trained and not allowed to run at large.

First you need to do your homework and locate breeders who produce the type of Aussie you are looking for. Speaking of which, what type will that be; a show dog, a pet/ companion or a working dog? Search for a breeder who is conscientious about matching his puppies to the right homes.

Sometimes there is very little difference between a show quality puppy and another puppy of good quality. The breeder may consider one puppy a pet quality when in fact it may lack only flashy markings, have an incorrect ear set or, possibly, a shorter coat.

It is important that Aussie puppies have time to play with their littermates in order to learn how to interact with other dogs later in life.

A healthy puppy who is sound can still participate in agility, obedience, tracking, flyball, Frisbee® and working trials. If it is just a companion or pet that the buyer is looking for, then the main concern should be to choose a well-socialized, healthy puppy with an excellent personality.

Good breeders spend countless hours observing their puppies in play. Each puppy will have a personality of its own and the breeder will want to help you select the one that best suits your personality and lifestyle.

The puppy's ancestry will indicate its potential temperament. Whenever possible, observe the father of the litter (if he is on the premises) in addition to the mother. The mother's temperament can have a major impact on the puppies, as they observe and learn from her behavior. If the mother is confident and well adjusted, the puppies are more likely to have a better start than if the mother is afraid.

Other factors also greatly influence behavior. The environment, socialization and the age at which the puppy goes to its new home all come into play. Socialization is critical. The ideal time for a puppy to go to his new home is at eight weeks of age. A puppy can be purchased at any time after that with equal success providing that the breeder has given necessary attention to socialization. A puppy removed from the litter too soon (prior to seven weeks) can suffer from inappropriate socialization to other dogs because he has not had the benefit of learning how to interact with his mother and littermates. On the other hand, a puppy that has not been properly exposed and socialized to friendly humans after the twelfth or thirteenth week will not form the necessary bond with humans to be an ideal companion.

Socialize your Australian Shepherd puppy with people and animals. A well-socialized puppy will get along with anybody or anything! This is Tyler Taylor, with friends.

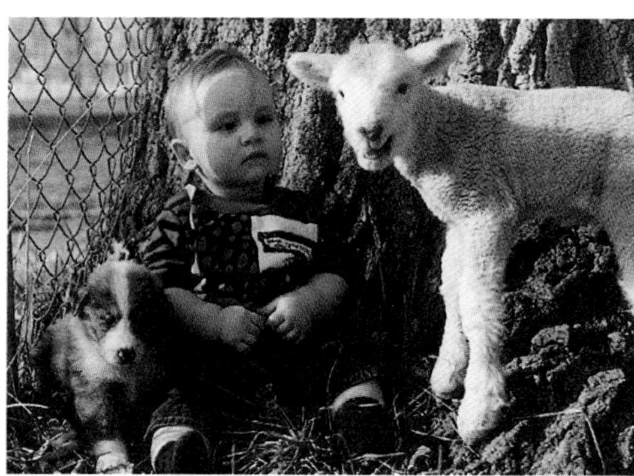

Once a suitable litter of Aussies has been located, each puppy must be considered, as each personality will differ even though each closely resembles its littermates. Upon examining the entire litter, it will be obvious that some of the puppies are more outgoing and will readily greet new visitors or engage in play with other puppies. Other puppies may appear less outgoing.

When studying a litter for the most suitable puppy, keep in mind that there is not just one "best" puppy. The "pick" of the litter is that puppy that is best suited for you and your family's lifestyle. The potential personality and temperament must compliment the potential owners in order for there to be a long-lasting and harmonious relationship. A dominant, aggressive Aussie with a high energy level is hardly a suitable companion for a meek owner with small children.

Dominant and submissive personalities joined by soft or hard characters all must be weighed out, because these types of Aussies require assertive owners. Mild-mannered, sensitive puppies need gentler handling.

There are basic personality tests that can be given to help determine the future personality of each puppy.

Each puppy can be placed on its back one at a time and held there for 30 seconds or so. Does the pup struggle to the end of the test, does it struggle a little bit and then relax or does it immediately submit and stay put?

When you squat down and without a word pet the puppy being considered, does he act content and enjoy the attention or does he cower or back away from you? Does he jump all over you and attack your hand? When you get up and walk away from the puppy, does he follow you or does he go the opposite way?

To see how quickly each puppy recovers from being startled and resumes with its activities, you can drop a tin can filled with pebbles or bang on a metal pie tin with a spoon.

The puppy that struggles to get away when on its back, jumps all over you and attacks your hands and legs may be too dominant for an inexperienced trainer or first-time owner. Overly shy or fearful puppies will require much socialization and patience. An extremely timid puppy hiding or cringing in the corner could become a fear biter.

For the most part, a puppy that struggles when placed on its back but then relaxes is demonstrating that it is willing to accept human authority. The puppy that readily follows a human is willing to allow the human to be the leader. When the puppy enjoys being petted he will look forward to and desire human companionship. And any puppy that quickly recovers from a sudden surprise is fairly confident and going to adjust quickly to new situations.

Since the breeder knows his Aussies better than anyone else, it is important to listen to his or her recommendations regarding your choice of a puppy. The breeder can give valuable insight on the potential character of each puppy, the degree of dominance, activity level, friendliness or fearfulness as the breeder has observed the litter in all phases of development and socialization.

There are two fragile stages of development that will require careful handling so as not to damage the pup's development. The first is between eight and twelve weeks and the second is between five and eight months of age.

The prospect of acquiring an older youngster or adult Aussie will be more appealing for some families. An adult or older youngster that is already crate trained, housebroken, walks on a leash and responds to basic obedience may be a better choice than a puppy who will require much attention during the first few months.

Interact with each individual puppy alone before deciding which to take home. The Australian Shepherd puppy you choose should be bright-eyed, healthy and happy.

When considering an older puppy or adult it is important to interact with the individual to see how well you get along and how the dog responds to walking on a leash, gentle handling and grooming, having you take away a bone or toy and gently holding its muzzle. You will have to rely on the breeder for insight on the dog's potential and to teach you how to properly handle and become acquainted with him.

A reputable breeder will be honest to assure the proper placement of his bloodline. A good breeder will have experience and knowledge about the breed and be willing to work with you in the event you require further assistance regarding the proper training and handling of your puppy.

Before you make your final decision, keep in mind that a healthy puppy will be active (providing it hasn't just woken up from a nap). The coat will be clean and free from inflamed skin and hair loss, which suggests external parasites such as mange, fleas and ringworm.

The ears should be free from crusty tips, indicating sarcoptic mange. Waxy ear canals and foul-smelling debris suggest ear mites. The gums should be bright pink, not red and inflamed or pale, indicating anemia or intestinal parasites. A hacking cough may suggest a respiratory infection (kennel cough) or even parasites.

A bulging navel indicates an umbilical hernia. Puppies often grow out of this or it may require minor surgery to repair. A good breeder will be aware of this and point this out prior to selling such an individual.

Breeders should supply the puppy's health records indicating when the puppy received appropriate vaccinations, was wormed and needed any other medical care. In Aussies, excessive white coat color should be avoided due to the defects associated with the homozygous dominant state of the merle gene.

The parents should be free from hip dysplasia (which causes lameness and

To ensure against genetic diseases and to preserve the quality of their programs, reputable breeders will screen all Australian Shepherds before breeding them.

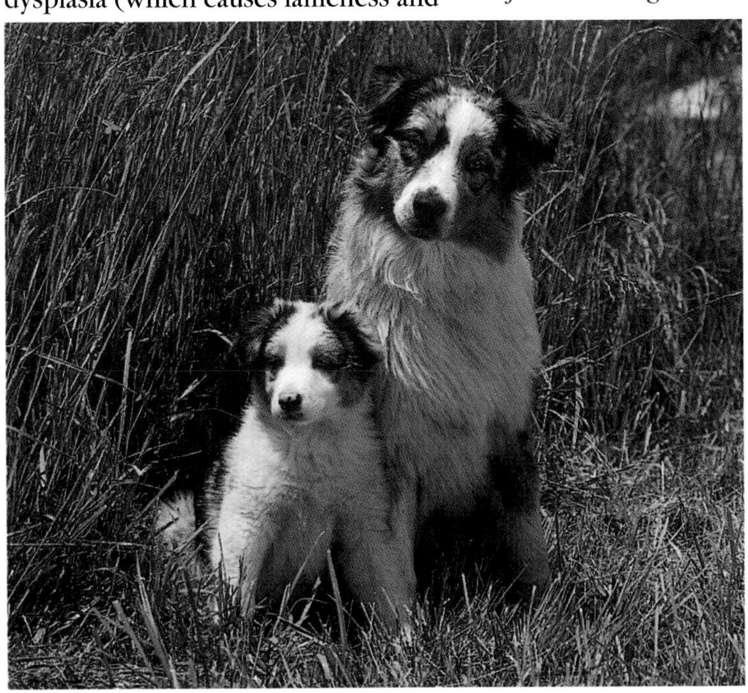

premature arthritis) and they should be free from inherited eye defects that can be passed to the puppies. Find out the breeder's policy regarding a health guarantee. Most reputable breeders will either replace a puppy, refund the purchase price or make an adjustment from the original purchase price. It is unreasonable to expect the breeder to guarantee your puppy against every possible health problem indefinitely. The breeder will probably require you to take your puppy to your veterinarian within 24 to 78 hours after leaving the premises to verify the state of the puppy's health. Congenital defects such as hip or eye problems will probably be guaranteed against should they surface by a certain date.

Take your Aussie puppy to the veterinarian for vaccinations and deworming as soon as possible, not only for your puppy's health, but for the health of your family as well.

It is important for the buyer to beware and ask the breeder any questions regarding the puppy's health, guarantees and ancestry prior to the purchase. A little time spent doing homework to locate an Australian Shepherd that matches all of your expectations will be more than worthwhile.

Besides the health guarantee, the purchaser will want to ask any questions regarding the registration and pedigree of the puppy. Aussies can be registered in any one of five different associations. In order for the puppy to be eligible to compete in a particular association, both parents must be registered with that association as well. The breeder should be able to show you the registration certificates proving the puppy's eligibility.

The puppy's pedigree is the puppy's family tree. Just because the puppy is pedigreed does not mean that it is registered. Nevertheless, the pedigree will indicate ancestry so that the owner can trace the known background and be better able to anticipate the future appearance, size and temperament of the litter. In addition, the ancestors' performance record, titles and genetic patterns can be researched.

The breeder should supply a three- to five-generation pedigree. Besides a certified pedigree, the breeder should provide either registration papers or applications when the puppy is paid in full. If the registration papers are not available when you acquire your Aussie, you should have them within a few months depending upon the association. The breeder should indicate the status of papers regarding with which association(s) the parents and litter are registered.

Any stipulations regarding papers should be fully discussed prior to purchasing the puppy. Questions should be answered, such as: Is there an additional fee for registration? Will the puppy be owned outright? And are there any limitations placed on the puppy (breeding or non-breeding quality)?

It is easy to fall in love with the beautiful Australian Shepherd puppy. Just make sure the decision to buy is a carefully considered and responsible one.

Each bloodline will have slightly different developmental patterns. Generally speaking, the Aussie will experience a loss of puppy coat as it nears four months of age and the adult guard hairs begin to come in. At some time, most all Aussie puppies get leggy and go through a gangly stage. As the head develops, the top jaw may grow a little longer than the bottom jaw, making the puppy appear slightly overshot between five and seven months of age. When the young Aussie develops its adult teeth, its ear-set can go up or down (higher or lower than its original set) during this time. When the puppy teethes, the ears can go all different directions. The breeder should be able to lend valuable insight as to the parents' ear sets and demonstrate to the buyer techniques of setting the ears, should that be necessary.

Most breeders will tell you the Aussie puppy will mature to look like the adult version of what it looks like between eight and twelve weeks of age. Some bloodlines are slower to mature than others, which is where the breeder and owners of each bloodline can help predict the growth patterns for a particular bloodline.

All puppies go through an awkward stage, but your Australian Shepherd pup should look a lot like his parents, only smaller.

CARING for Your Australian Shepherd

ne of the pleasures of owning an Australian Shepherd is that its coat does not require heavy grooming (providing it is the correct texture). Aussies are subject to seasonal shedding, and unspayed females usually shed approximately a couple of months after their heat cycle or having a litter of puppies.

The Aussie's double coat, which consists of a downy, water-resistant coat next to the skin and thicker, longer guard hairs on top, requires a thorough weekly brushing to stay clean and healthy by removing any dead hair. When shedding, a light brushing two or three times a week will cut down on stray hairs throughout the house or automobile.

GROOMING YOUR AUSTRALIAN SHEPHERD

A good pin brush with smooth, blunt-tipped metal pins secured in a rubber pad is a must. When your Aussie starts to shed, brush the entire coat to remove dead hair and distribute natural oils. Gently brush from the ends down to the skin to stimulate circulation and to remove dust and dry skin. Grooming spray reduces static and moisturizes the coat, giving it greater elasticity.

If you find a mat, gently untangle the hair with your fingers and a medium-toothed comb. Mats can be difficult to unsnarl. A few drops of a detangler/conditioner may help to relax the knot.

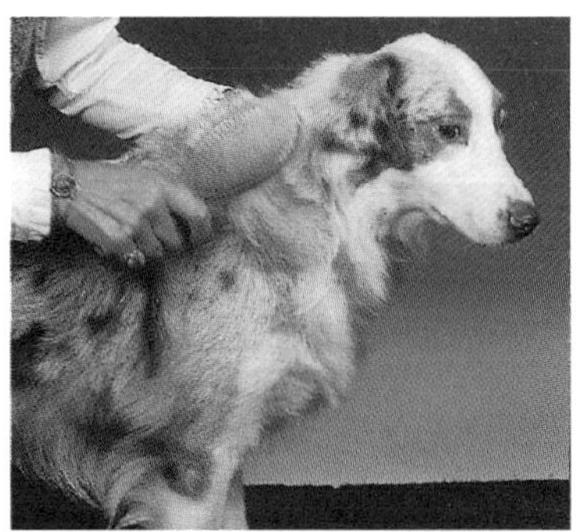

An Australian Shepherd does not require extensive grooming, but a thorough weekly brushing will remove any dead hairs and prevent heavy shedding.

If you accustom your Aussie to being groomed it will become a pleasurable experience for both of you. This handsome boy is Hall of Fame Sire Ch. Las Rocosa Little Wolf.

Stubborn mats will need to be cut out. You must take care not to cut the skin in the process. Gently work the comb between the mat and alongside the skin.

To get your Aussie accustomed to being brushed, it is best to start with short sessions (five to ten minutes). Gradually lengthen the sessions. The Aussie can sit, stand or lie down at your side or in your lap, on the floor or on a rubber-matted table at waist height.

If your Aussie is reluctant to allow you to brush him, be persistent, but patient. Kind handling will teach him to accept and enjoy the experience. This should be pleasant quality time for both dog and owner. It is not necessary to bathe your Aussie more than once every few months unless you are showing him or he develops an unpleasant odor or gets dirty. Always brush before bathing. Once the coat is thoroughly brushed, you can wet it. If you bathe your Aussie without brushing first, the coat can become entangled and matted, making it extremely difficult to comb.

The underside of the ear flaps should be gently cleansed with a mild ear-cleansing solution. Don't probe into the ear canal where you cannot see. Place cotton in the ears to prevent water from entering the ear canal during the bath.

A drop of mineral oil should be placed in the eyes to avoid irritation from shampoo, unless using a tearless shampoo pH balanced for dogs. The pH balance is important to leave the coat shiny and manageable. If the hair is dry, a mild conditioner can be used during the bath process. A dab of Vaseline can be gently rubbed on the nose leather to keep it supple.

After completely rinsing all the soap residue from the hair, towel-dry the coat by blotting out excess water. The coat is then ready to be brushed and blown dry.

Regular grooming is also important to control external parasites, especially fleas and ticks. Flea bites can induce allergic reactions in some Aussies, which can be painful and lead to a bacterial infection. Grooming also gives the owner an opportunity to discover potential problems such as cuts, lumps and abscesses from burrs penetrating the skin before they require medical attention. Weed seeds and stickers can migrate in the ear canal, the eyelid or even a nostril. Mud, tar, burrs and ice can collect between the foot pads and must be removed to alleviate irritation and injury. Any foul odors or discharges from an affected area may require a veterinarian's attention.

The Aussie's feet should be inspected and, if necessary, the toenails should be shortened. Unless worn down from work and exercise, the toenail can become injured or torn off. The base of the toenail can get infected, causing great discomfort to the dog. Also, when the nails are too long, they can cause the foot to spread out, making it more prone to injury. Trim a little length off at a time. Aussies may or may not have front

When showing your Australian Shepherd, learn how to groom him to accentuate his strong points.

dewclaws (the fifth toe on the inside of the leg by the pastern). These need to be kept trimmed so they don't curl around and imbed in the leg.

An Aussie's feet must be inspected regularly for injuries and his toenails kept short to prevent any tearing or discomfort.

Grooming for the Show Ring

The stray hair on the back of the hocks, pasterns, around the paws, around the bobbed tail and on the top of the ears should be trimmed to give a neater overall appearance. Use blunt-nosed scissors to trim with. Whiskers may or may not be trimmed. The coat can be misted with water or grooming spray, brushed and blown dry so the hair lays in the most complimentary lines to enhance the

These Aussies love their baby pool. An affection for water bodes well for bath time!

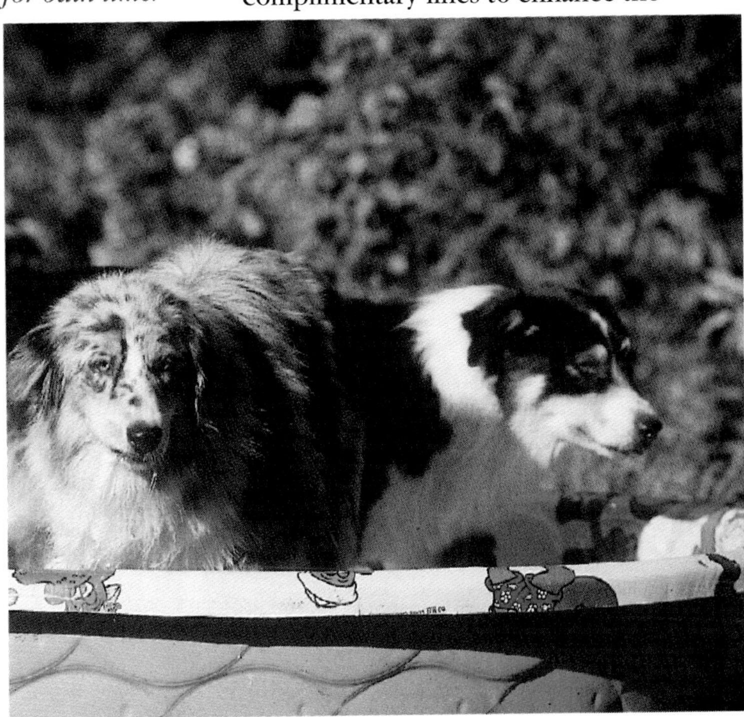

overall conformation. Any small structural faults can be minimized or "camouflaged" with brushing techniques. For instance, if the Aussie has a weak or sagging topline, the haircoat can be blown against the grain to "fill out" the dip or low area. A dog with finer bone can be made to look like it has adequate bone by brushing the hair up on the feet and legs. Your Aussie's breeder will help you determine the structural strong points and weaknesses and teach you how to best prepare him for the show ring.

EXERCISING YOUR AUSTRALIAN SHEPHERD

Like all dogs born to work, Aussies need daily exercise. They can get adequate exercise if they have a large enough yard to play in, but they are not as likely to run and play by themselves. The companionship of another dog may encourage a good hard run if they play and chase each other around the yard.

For most Aussies it is up to the owner to provide the outlet for exercise and play. Ideally, herding is the ultimate form of exercise, but when this is not possible, a simple agility obstacle course can also provide lots of entertainment and exercise for both the owner and Aussie.

Swimming is excellent exercise, but so is a nice walk combined with a retrieving game with a ball, Frisbee® or other toy. An Aussie exercised off leash will cover three times the distance running around his owner than one who is walked right next to his owner on leash. The new flexible leashes are good choices to use when leash laws are in effect or to maintain the dog's safety–and even the safety of others.

The exercise program should be structured to the Aussie's age and physical fitness. In the course of a day, puppies require

An Australian Shepherd needs lots of exercise and activity. It is your job as his owner to provide him an outlet for entertainment and play.

approximately a half-mile or so of exercise and play.

Puppies are not geared for a strict program of activities. Exercise and play are important to the developing youngster, but forced exercise can hurt the puppy more than help him when the bones are still soft.

The Gumabone® Frisbee® is a great toy for your Australian Shepherd. They are available at all pet shops* *The trademark Frisbee is used under license from Mattel, Inc., CA, USA.

If the owner wants to enter his or her Aussie in competition, it will be necessary to provide additional activity to increase stamina and improve muscle tone. Your Aussie should be exercised four to five times a week for at least a month prior to heavy training and competition to increase physical and mental stamina. Exercise no less than three days a week will maintain your dog's present condition. Heavy exercise–six to seven times a week–can actually be detrimental, as the body needs time to rest and heal, which promotes good health.

Road work can begin at one-eighth to one-quarter of a mile for the first few days, then be gradually built up to a half a mile or so until by the end of the month you and your Aussie can comfortably do a couple of miles. This not only encourages good muscle tone for the dog, but there are additional benefits for the owner as well. The owner can walk briskly or run beside the dog.

When jogging on cement or pavement, the distances should be decreased because the hard surfaces can cause lameness and cause the Aussie's feet and pasterns to break down. If the dog becomes lame or stiff, let him rest and heal for several days. Once recovered, resume the program more slowly. When the desired muscle tone and stamina is achieved, you can decrease the exercise program to three times a week by alternating heavy exercise and training with light play and satisfying walks.

In a hot, humid part of the country, it may be necessary to exercise your Aussie in the cooler part of the day. It is also important to gradually build up the length of activity so as not to overexert your dog. A dog loses heat by panting. It cannot sweat as humans do, except through its pads. If the heat gets built up and the dog cannot adequately get rid of this excess heat by panting, the body temperature rises and the dog becomes overheated. If this condition progresses and is not altered, the dog may collapse and can die. Be careful to make sure you are not pushing the dog beyond its limits. If it becomes exhausted or wants to stop or lie down during the session, you need to shorten the workouts.

There are danger signs you must recognize if your dog gets overheated: Staggering or heavy panting with bright red mucous membranes requires immediate, emergency attention. Quickly immerse the Aussie in *cool* water; ice-cold water can put your dog into shock. Pour cold water over your dog's head to reduce swelling of the brain. If you don't have anything to immerse the dog in water, pour water over the legs, under the belly and head. Allow him to lick ice cubes.

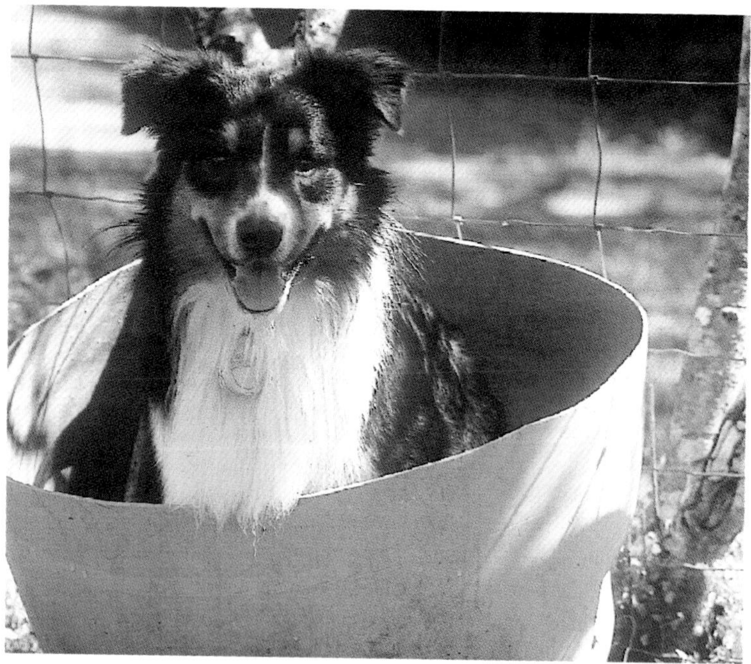

Give your Aussie plenty of cool, clean water after exercising in order to keep him well hydrated and to prevent heat exhaustion. He may choose to sit in it rather than drink it.

Dehydration is always a threat from hard work and heavy exercise. The lungs and liver become stressed by body heat and toxic wastes, cell loss is caused by friction and important vitamins and minerals become depleted. Electrolytes need to be replaced to balance the metabolism. Children's formula electrolytes can be added to drinking water. Your Aussie's normal body temperature is 100.5-102 degrees Fahrenheit, but is increased with activity. During times of heavy exercise avoid giving cold water as it can lead to stomach cramps. A light snack such as a small packet of semi-moist dog food, hard boiled eggs, chicken or rice balls can boost your Aussie's energy level.

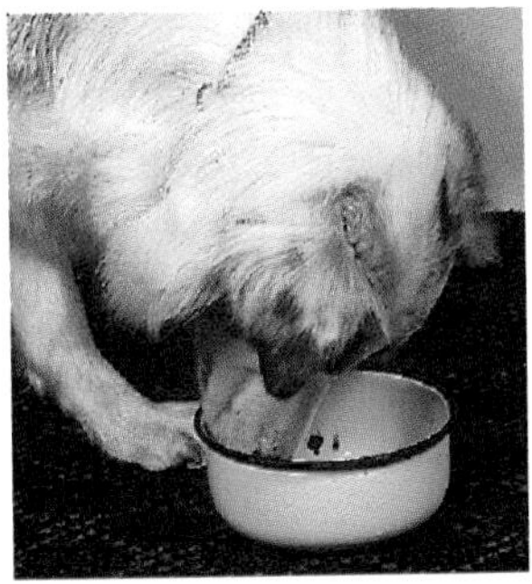

A light snack can boost your Australian Shepherd's energy level after a heavy workout.

Heavy exercise can put wear and tear on the feet. Before the dog gets into shape, his pads are rough, but eventually smooth out and get thinner. The areas between the toes, the webs of the feet, can get cracked and injured by sharp rocks and burrs.

Pad-toughening agents can be applied as a preventative measure. Leather dog booties can be used to protect sore or injured feet. They must fit properly to stay on, but not so tight that they cut off circulation and hinder normal foot movements. Boots should always be taken off during rest periods to allow the foot to breathe and restore normal circulation should it be slightly hindered. To get your Aussie used to wearing the boots, put them on during play times. It will take several times of wearing the boots to get accustomed to them.

Injured feet should be treated by cleansing the wounds with a mild antiseptic. Deep cuts need sutures to help the healing process.

Feeding Your Australian Shepherd

A proper diet is important for all phases of your Aussie's life and activities. Nutrition is important for good health.

Research and extensive feeding trials have been conducted

by major dog food companies to establish complete and balanced diets to provide necessary nutrients to meet the daily requirements for each stage of life. Choose a ration specifically formulated to meet the needs of your dog. These are growth (for puppies, growing youngsters and young adults), performance (for active Aussies, nursing mothers and working Aussies); maintenance (for adults), and senior (for the special needs of aging Aussies). If the bag does not state that it is complete and balanced, choose a different brand. While less expensive than a professional formula, generic formulas often contain inferior ingredients.

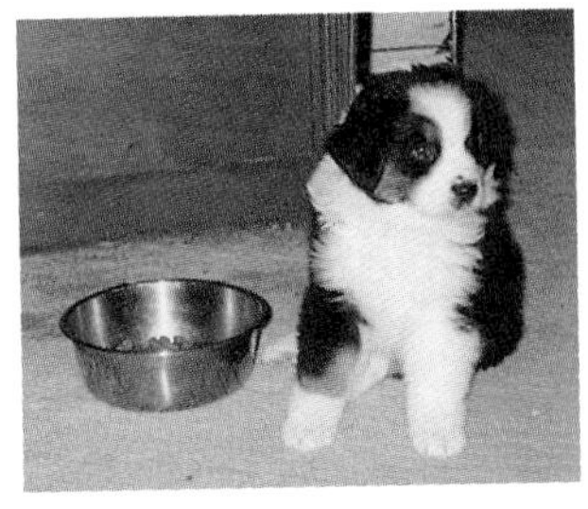

Choose a food for your Aussie based on his nutritional requirements for his specific stage of life. Puppies need a growth formula.

Supplements are unnecessary if the diet is adequate. Supplementing with extra vitamins and minerals can be detrimental and upset your Aussie's system when feeding a nutritionally balanced diet.

Always provide a clean source of fresh water. Water is the most important part of nutrition and necessary for all bodily functions.

Housing Your Australian Shepherd

Aussies need a safe play area, secure yard, fenced kennel run or puppy-proof room when you are unable to be with them. The accommodations must be comfortable and free from environmental dangers (poisonous substances, electric shock and weather extremes). Aussies, like all dogs, need adequate ventilation and shade in warm weather, and shelter from the wind, rains, and snow in cold, damp weather. They need a fresh supply of clean water in all weather. No matter how elaborate or simple the accommodations, the ultimate requirement for Australian Shepherds is to spend quality time in the company of their owners everyday to keep their spirits high.

Aussies need a safe haven from the elements and a place to call their own. Provide adequate shelter for your dog if he is to be outside for long periods of time.

TRAINING Your Australian Shepherd

Because of their heritage, Aussies are free thinkers and may appear as though they are trying to defy or outwit their owners. Aussies are eager to please, and any owner who misreads his dog's mind and tries to force it into submission can destroy the breed's high spirit and enthusiasm. Aussies excel and learn easily with owners who use positive motivational techniques. The only requirement in training an Aussie is that the owner must be flexible in his teaching. The rough or abusive approach to training generally occurs out of a lack of knowledge or when the owner tries to get immediate results by taking a short cut in training.

If you are a patient and flexible teacher, your Australian Shepherd is smart enough to learn even the most difficult of tricks.

Reward training or positive reinforcement is far superior to punishment training. Reward training produces better results because the Aussie learns quicker with more motivation and retains the lessons. Positive play training is one of the best forms of motivational training. Play training transforms conventional methods of teaching dry obedience exercises or stock dog commands (when no livestock is available) into exciting, innovative ones. Ultimately, the owner creates an attitude that enables each Aussie to perform his lessons with excitement and enthusiasm—something that cannot be taught through intimidation or negative corrections.

In order to get the respect of your Aussie, you must be fair in your teaching and realistic in your expectations. Too often owners tend to teach too many lessons to the dog at the same time without giving him a chance to absorb the previous

If you begin training your Australian Shepherd early, he will grow to become a valued member of your family.

lesson. No two Aussies are alike, nor will they act identical or learn at the same rate. You need to take your Aussie's environment and your experience (or lack of it) into consideration in order to develop him to his fullest potential.

Since a puppy's brain is fully developed when he is seven weeks of age, gentle training can begin immediately. One of the first and most important lessons the Aussie puppy can learn is housebreaking. The ideal way to housebreak an Aussie puppy is simply to anticipate his needs and take him outside before an accident occurs in the house. Immediately after the puppy wakes up from a nap, first thing in the morning, the last thing before going to bed at night and after he drinks or eats, he needs to go outside. If the owner is alert and aware he will take the puppy outside to an appropriate spot to establish the good habit of voiding outside instead of inside the house.

Housebreaking is often most successfully accomplished by using a puppy crate (a travel kennel, plastic, wire or wooden crate). When properly introduced to a crate, Aussie puppies adapt to them very successfully. Proper introduction to the crate means using the crate for only brief periods of time when you are unable to keep an eye on the puppy. A crate should be thought of like a playpen for a child. Aussies, like all dogs, are den animals by nature and regard the crate as private space.

A crate should be chosen that allows the puppy to stand up and lie down comfortably–not too big or too small. Because an Aussie wants to keep his den or sleeping place clean, his natural inclination will be to void as far away from it as possible. Just prior to crating, take the puppy outside and allow him to relieve himself, then give him a treat and place him in the crate. If the puppy seems anxious and barks or whines, ignore him until he stops. If necessary, leave the room. The puppy will learn that you won't run and let him out every time he barks. Within a few days, the puppy will accept being crated for brief periods and at night when you are sleeping.

The crate is an excellent place to feed the puppy his dinner. Just as soon as the puppy has finished supper, take him outside so he can do his business. When you bring the puppy back in the house leave the crate door open so he can come and go, as long as you are alert to when he will need to void. Take him out each and every time he sniffs around the floor and walks in circles. Within a week you will see how easily the Aussie puppy goes to the same door you have taken him in and out of to do his business. As long as you are always alert to his needs he should not backslide in his housetraining–providing he is not sick. Soon his bladder and bowels will become stronger and rather than taking him out every two hours, you can leave him in the house for three to four hours before an accident occurs.

All Aussies need to be leash trained. Training with a leash is easy and should be an enjoyable experience for both owner and puppy. Put a buckle collar on the puppy, making sure it is loose enough to allow you to get two fingers under the collar, but not so loose that it slips off when the puppy bulks against the collar and gets free. Never leave the collar on the puppy unless you are present; the collar could get caught or hung up and the puppy could easily choke should this occur. Attach a light leash to the collar and allow the puppy to drag this around the room or fenced-in yard. Once the puppy gets used to having the collar on after several different days of dragging the leash in your presence for 10 or 15 minutes at a time, he will not scratch at the collar or seem to take notice.

A collar and leash are essential tools to begin your Australian Shepherd's training sessions. All Aussies need to be leash trained for their safety and the safety of others.

With the leash in hand, encourage the puppy to follow you. A piece of cheese or hot dog are good motivators to "lure" the puppy in your direction. If the puppy bulks at the leash, don't jerk it, but loosen the leash and continue to entice him with the treat. When the puppy reaches towards the treat, back away and call the puppy with an encouraging tone of voice. After the first couple of sessions back away more quickly, encouraging the puppy to follow without hesitation. Make a game out of the lesson. Each session will be regarded as fun and play for the puppy, when in fact you are shaping the puppy with little resistance.

Once the puppy is walking comfortably on a leash you can take him for daily walks without worrying about him running away or getting hit by a car. A puppy will easily get distracted, and can get into the habit of not returning when you call him. On different occasions when walking on the leash, the owner can practice calling the puppy and backing quickly away. When the puppy responds the owner should praise him and can offer a food treat every now and then to reinforce the response. Food treats can be used for a favorable response.

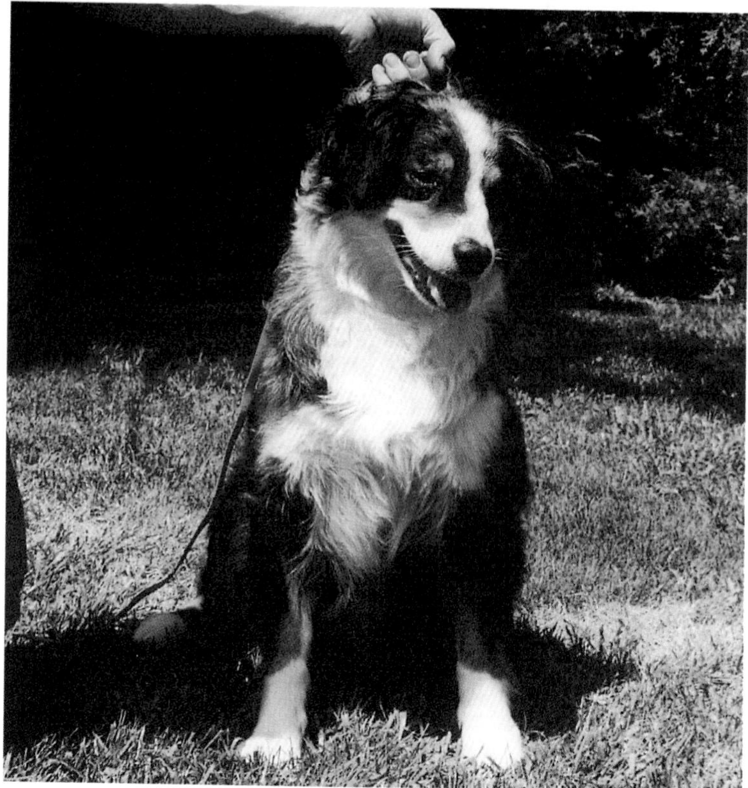

Use the training collar to remind your Australian Shepherd what you want him to do; for example, sit. Las Rocosa Blue Diamond is getting the picture.

They should not, however, be the sole reward. They should be used in the beginning while teaching the puppy, but then should be mixed with attention and petting by the owner. Always verbally enforce each command so your puppy understands acceptable from unacceptable behavior. Always praise the puppy for coming when you call it and then reward it with a treat or attention. Offer the treat less often as he learns what to do. Always give verbal praise and attention for good behavior.

Aussies are so intelligent that practice makes perfect. Be sure to follow through with every command you give. You must keep in mind that you need to be clear in the commands you give your Aussie.

In order to correct your Aussie from doing what you don't want, you must catch him just as he begins to respond incorrectly or misbehave. In other words, when you call your puppy to come to you once you have gently taught him that coming is a rewarding experience, you can quickly snap the slack out of the leash and walk away from the puppy if he doesn't respond or goes the other direction. When the puppy follows, praise and reward him. Never jerk the puppy harshly, but give a quick little tug at the leash and then let it go slack.

During this period of leash training take care to keep the training sessions fun and short. Gentle handling is also important during this time. The puppy needs to associate the leash with positive experiences as this will set the foundation for all other training and handling.

This is also the time for necessary socialization for the puppy. Lots of friendly people can be encountered, but on a gradual basis. This is especially important in the eighth week of a puppy's life. This early training and socialization is imperative in the Aussie's upbringing. Careful exposure to various people and places will make him more responsive to future training.

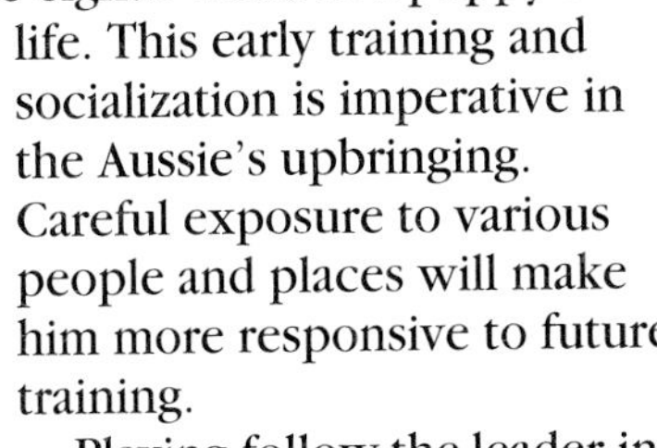

This well-socialized Aussie is perfectly comfortable with his buddies. His pleasant experiences make him more responsive to their training.

Playing follow-the-leader in leash training is twofold: It not only teaches the puppy to come to you when you call, but it establishes the owner as the leader of the pack, which is important to the puppy. Dogs are highly social animals and naturally respond to the pack structure. As pack leader you must be firm and clear when giving commands. Firmness must be balanced by praise and affection when the Aussie obeys. Although your Aussie is walking on a leash and coming and following when called, now you want to teach the puppy not to run ahead of you and take you for a walk instead. Every time the puppy pulls ahead, back away from the puppy. This will teach him to keep an eye on you. Be consistent. Don't let him tug on the leash sometimes and then correct him for tugging the next time.

With a treat in your hand you can lure your Aussie into a sitting position by holding the treat just above his nose. As the puppy lifts his head to sniff or reach for the food, you can continue to lift the treat upward and arch it over his head toward his rump. As he lifts his head up and back, his body is in an ideal position to allow you to guide him into sitting position with little or no resistance. You can also shape the puppy into a sitting position by gently tugging backwards on his collar and applying gentle pressure on his rump. Whenever asking the puppy to sit, always remember to praise and reward each response.

You must always be consistent with your commands when training your Australian Shepherd. Ch. Las Rocosa Justin Jr. Mount Gold is standing at attention.

This is Blue Lad Michigan Bobby obeying the down command given by his owner Scott George.

From the sitting position, the down can be taught. The puppy can simply be placed in a down by luring him downwards with the treat, drawing the food down and forward. If the puppy doesn't easily follow the food treat into the lying down position, you can use one hand to lure and the other one (placed over the puppy's shoulders) to gently push or guide the puppy down. Some puppies may need additional guidance by gently pulling the collar down and forward while the other hand places gentle pressure over the shoulders to place him down.

From both the sitting and down positions, the owner can teach the puppy to stay in place for a few seconds at a time. The leash will come in handy for these exercises. When the puppy offers no resistance to being placed in the down position, accompanied by saying the Aussie's name with the command "Down," the owner can place the leash under his or her foot and tell the puppy "Stay." When the puppy gets up to move, the leash will remind the puppy to stay. When the owner steps on the leash it should not be tight to hold the Aussie down, but with an inch or so of slack to check the puppy. Enforce this with a clear, concise "Stay." After a brief wait, you can tell the puppy "OK" to let him know he is free to get up.

Practice the stay from a sitting position by telling him to stay, but instead of standing on the leash, take the leash in your hand and, if the puppy tries to follow, give him a quick tug backwards and repeat the command "Stay." Vary the duration that you ask the puppy to stay, and at first only step out in front of the puppy. Gradually move farther and farther away.

The stay command can be applied in many different applications. It is important for your Aussie to stand to allow you to groom him, for the vet to examine him, and for obedience competition and the show ring. The command "Stand" can be given any time you are brushing your Aussie. If he tries to sit, you can gently tickle him under his belly. Ask him to stand for short periods of time only.

The stand command can be practiced from both the sit and down positions. When the Aussie is sitting you can gently draw his collar forward while placing your hand underneath to tickle his belly. Don't forget the praise and reward for responding.

A puppy kindergarten class is an ideal way to socialize your puppy with other puppies and people. It is also a good way to receive guidance from an experienced trainer to help develop your handling skills and teach proper training techniques.

The basic obedience exercises are good for Aussies in all phases of life and competition. Whether a pet, obedience competitor, working dog or showdog, obedience is necessary to communicate basic desires. All basic skills can be fine-tuned to meet the needs of different activities. There is one thing that must be considered: In many obedience classes, the dogs are trained according to competitive obedience. In competition, dogs are judged on how well they stay at their owner's side. In training for obedience competition dogs get praised for being at their owner's sides. You cannot expect that an Aussie trained this way will feel at ease to move away from you if he has been corrected every time for doing so in the past, unless you teach him that there are times when it is okay to do so. This is especially important in livestock training.

Training your Australian Shepherd will be fun and rewarding for both of you. The time spent training will lay the foundation for a lasting and unconditional relationship.

Training the Australian Shepherd for Herding

Most Australian Shepherds are born with an inherent desire to herd. The trait is readily recognized when young puppies are observed nipping at their master's heels as they are walking. People who do not understand that the young puppy is attempting to herd often think this is a vicious attempt to bite and will reprimand the puppy harshly, doing irreparable damage to the young puppy's mind. A young dog that is going to be used for herding work should never be hit or beaten. If he is in a bad situation, simply remove the puppy from the situation and prevent the incident from happening again.

A young dog needs to be socialized and become familiar to places and things around his premises. He needs to have public exposure to people,

An Aussie uses the "eyeing" technique to herd sheep. The ability to move stock with such stealth is an inherited trait in the Australian Shepherd.

noises, and other dogs if he is to reach his full potential as a herding dog. As your young Australian Shepherd develops, he will show tendencies to want to herd livestock when he sees them, either in a pen or in a pasture lot. We call this stage of development being ready to run, meaning that he is now ready to be introduced to the world of herding.

There are a number of important steps you must take before you expose your dog to livestock and let him come into contact with them. I would not recommend that you turn an overly enthusiastic dog loose on a bunch of cattle for fear he could be severely injured by being kicked or trampled. Often such an experience can ruin a dog for life. For the novice handler, sheep are a lot safer to work with . Here again, it's important to select gentle sheep, not wild or flighty ones that the young dog cannot come into contact with. Nor do you want to expose your young dog to sheep that will get into a corner and fight. Your dog will soon become discouraged and quit trying to herd them. White-faced sheep tend to flock together better than black-faced ones, which is a definite advantage for the dog just starting to herd.

Herding cattle can be very dangerous to your dog. Your Australian Shepherd must be carefully trained in herding to avoid any serious injury.

By selecting gentle sheep that move off of a dog easily, the next important thing is to be sure you have an adequate area in which to start working a young dog. To begin with, a good setup is a round pen that is approximately one hundred feet in diameter fenced with snow fence. Such an area is small enough to prevent the sheep from escaping, yet large enough to allow them to move off of the dog. After about six or eight lessons, if they are handled properly, it will be to your advantage to move onto a larger area maybe one-half to one acre in size. With proper handling through these stages, you should, in due time, be ready for more extensive training.

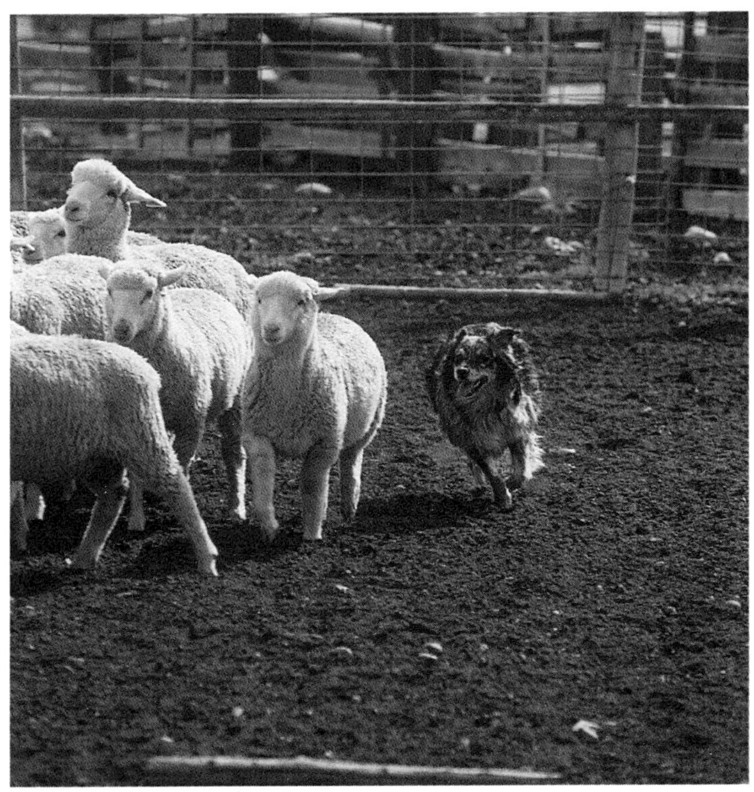

Socialize your Aussie with the animals he will be working with and slowly introduce your dog to the herding concept.

Whenever you are training your dog, there are a number of very important rules you must observe if you are to be successful. Never put your young dog in a situation where he may be mauled or injured. Never overwork your dog to the point that he becomes disinterested in herding. Never hit or beat your dog. Not all training sessions are progressive. If this happens, quit for the day. Do not push your dog beyond his capacity. Do not attempt to take shortcuts in your training program. Praise your dog for a job well done *after* the job or the training session is finished, not while he is doing it. If you follow these rules, work patiently with your dog and consult with experienced herders, you'll find that herding with your Australian Shepherd can be very rewarding and fun.

SPORT of Purebred Dogs

Welcome to the exciting and sometimes frustrating sport of dogs. No doubt you are trying to learn more about dogs or you wouldn't be deep into this book. This section covers the basics that may entice you, further your knowledge and help you to understand the dog world. If you decide to give showing, obedience or any other dog activities a try, then I suggest you seek further help from the appropriate source.

Dog showing has been a very popular sport for a long time and has been taken quite seriously by some. Others only enjoy it as a hobby.

The Kennel Club in England was formed in 1859, the American Kennel Club was established in 1884 and the Canadian Kennel Club was formed in 1888. The purpose of these clubs was to register purebred dogs and maintain their Stud Books. In the beginning, the concept of registering dogs was not readily accepted. More than 36 million dogs have been enrolled in the AKC Stud Book since its inception in 1888. Presently the kennel clubs not only register dogs but adopt and enforce rules and regulations governing dog shows, obedience trials and field trials. Over the years they have fostered and encouraged interest in the health and welfare of the purebred dog. They routinely donate funds to veterinary research for study on genetic disorders.

Following are the addresses of the kennel clubs in the United States, Great Britain and Canada.

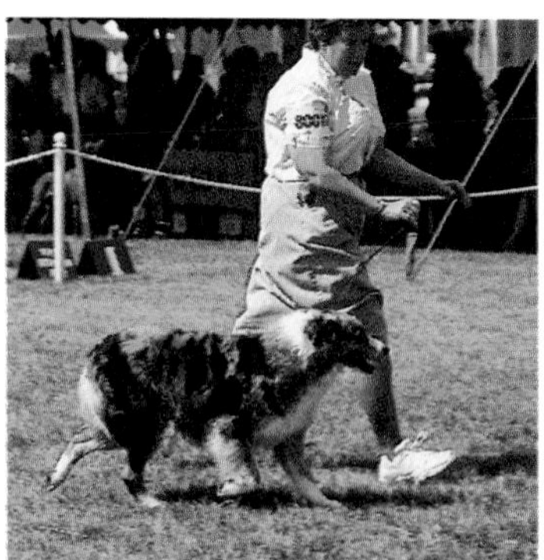

Conformation showing is just one activity you can compete in with a versatile Aussie.

An array of champions in a variety of colors. Owner, Lorreine McLean.

The American Kennel Club
51 Madison Avenue
New York, NY 10010
(Their registry is located at: 5580 Centerview Drive, STE 200, Raleigh, NC 27606-3390)

The Kennel Club
1 Clarges Street
Piccadilly, London, WIY 8AB, England

The Canadian Kennel Club
111 Eglinton Avenue
East Toronto, Ontario M6S 4V7
Canada

Today there are numerous activities that are enjoyable for both the dog and the handler. Some of the activities include conformation showing, obedience competition, tracking, agility, the Canine Good Citizen Certificate, and a wide range of instinct tests that vary from breed to breed. Where you start depends upon your goals which early on may not be readily apparent.

PUPPY KINDERGARTEN

Every puppy will benefit from this class. PKT is the foundation for all future dog activities from conformation to "couch potatoes." Pet owners should make an effort to attend even if they never expect to show their dog. The class is designed for puppies about three months of age with graduation at approximately five months of age. All the puppies will be in the same age group and, even though some may be a little unruly, there should not be any real problem. This class will teach the puppy some beginning obedience. As in all obedience classes the owner learns how to train his own dog. The PKT class gives the puppy the opportunity to interact with other puppies in the same age group and exposes him to strangers, which is very important. Some dogs grow up with behavior problems, one of them being fear of strangers. As you can see, there can be much to gain from this class.

There are some basic obedience exercises that every dog should learn. Some of these can be started with puppy kindergarten.

Sit

One way of teaching the sit is to have your dog on your left side with the leash in your right hand, close to the collar. Pull up on the leash and at the same time reach around his hindlegs with your left hand and tuck them in. As you are doing this say, "Beau, sit." Always use the dog's name when you give an active command. Some owners like to use a treat holding it over the dog's head. The dog will need to sit to get the treat. Encourage the dog to hold the sit for a few seconds, which will eventually be the beginning of the Sit/Stay. Depending on how cooperative he is, you can rub him under the chin or stroke his back. It is a good time to establish eye contact.

Down

Sit the dog on your left side and kneel down beside him with the leash in your right hand. Reach over him with your left hand and grasp his left foreleg. With your right hand, take his right foreleg and pull his legs forward while you say, "Beau, down." If he tries to get up, lean on his shoulder to encourage him to stay down. It will relax your dog if you stroke his back while he is down. Try to encourage him to stay down for a few seconds as preparation for the Down/Stay.

Heel

The definition of heeling is the dog walking under control at your left heel. Your puppy will learn controlled walking in the puppy kindergarten class, which will eventually lead to heeling. The command is "Beau, heel," and you start off briskly with your left foot. Your leash is in your right hand and your left hand is holding it about half way down. Your left hand should be able to control the leash and there should be a little slack in it. You want him to walk with you with your leg somewhere between his nose and his shoulder. You need to encourage him to stay with you, not forging (in front of you) or lagging behind you. It is best to keep him on a fairly short lead. Do not allow the lead to become tight. It is far better to give him a little jerk when necessary and remind him to heel. When you come to a halt, be prepared physically to make him sit. It takes practice to become coordinated. There are excellent books on training that you may wish to purchase. Your instructor should be able to recommend one for you.

With persistence, patience and praise, your Australian Shepherd will soon be sitting at your command.

Recall

This quite possibly is the most important exercise you will ever teach. It should be a pleasant experience. The puppy may learn to do random recalls while being attached to a long line such as a clothes line. Later the exercise will start with the dog sitting and staying until called. The command is "Beau, come." Let your command be happy. You want your dog to come willingly and faithfully. The recall could save his life if he sneaks out the door. In practicing the recall, let him jump on you or touch you before you reach for him. If he is shy, then kneel down to his level. Reaching for the insecure dog could frighten him, and he may not be willing to come again in the future. Lots of praise and a treat would be in order whenever you do a recall. Under no circumstances should you ever correct your dog when he has come to you. Later in formal obedience your dog will be required to sit in front of you after recalling and then go to heel position.

Play is a great reward after practicing obedience exercises. This Aussie can't wait to get his Gumabone® Frisbee®.

** The tradmark Frisbee is used under license from Mattel, Inc. California, USA.*

CONFORMATION

Conformation showing is our oldest dog show sport. This type of showing is based on the dog's appearance–that is his structure, movement and attitude. When considering this type of showing, you need to be aware of your breed's standard and be able to evaluate your dog compared to that standard. The breeder of your puppy or other experienced breeders would be good sources for such an evaluation. Puppies can go through lots of changes over a period of time. I always say most puppies start out as promising hopefuls and then after maturing may be disappointing as show candidates. Even so this should not deter them from being excellent pets.

Usually conformation training classes are offered by the local kennel or obedience clubs. These are excellent places for training puppies. The puppy should be able to walk on a lead before entering such a class. Proper ring procedure and technique for posing (stacking) the

In a conformation show, the dog is judged on his appearance and how well he conforms to the standards of the breed.

Ch. Las Rocosa Tom Bull Wolf with owner and author Joesph Hartnagle.

dog will be demonstrated as well as gaiting the dog. Usually certain patterns are used in the ring such as the triangle or the "L." Conformation class, like the PKT class, will give your youngster the opportunity to socialize with different breeds of dogs and humans too.

It takes some time to learn the routine of conformation showing. Usually one starts at the puppy matches which may be AKC Sanctioned or Fun Matches. These matches are generally for puppies from two or three months to a year old, and there may be classes for the adult over the age of 12 months. Similar to point shows, the classes are divided by sex and after completion of the classes in that breed or variety, the class winners compete for Best of Breed or Variety. The winner goes on to compete in the Group and the Group winners compete for Best in Match. No championship points are awarded for match wins.

A few matches can be great training for puppies even though there is no intention to go on showing. Matches enable the puppy to meet new people and be handled by a stranger—the judge. It is also a change of environment, which broadens the horizon for both dog and handler. Matches and other dog activities boost the confidence of the handler and especially the younger handlers.

Earning an AKC championship is built on a point system, which is different from Great Britain. To become an AKC Champion of Record the dog must earn 15 points. The number of points earned each time depends upon the number of dogs in competition. The number of points available at each show depends upon the breed, its sex and the location of the show. The United States is divided into ten AKC zones. Each zone has its own set of points. The purpose of the zones is to try to equalize the points available from breed to breed and area to area.The AKC adjusts the point scale annually.

This is Ch. Las Rocosa Wyo Meo, owned by Anita Simon-Laycock winning Best of Breed.

The number of points that can be won at a show are between one and five. Three-, four- and five-point wins are considered majors. Not only does the dog need 15 points won under three different judges, but those points must include two majors under two different judges. Canada also works on a point system but majors are not required.

Dogs always show before bitches. The classes available to those seeking points are: Puppy (which may be divided into 6 to 9 months and 9 to 12 months); 12 to 18 months; Novice; Bred-by-Exhibitor; American-bred; and Open. The class winners of the same sex of each breed or variety compete against each other for Winners Dog and Winners Bitch. A Reserve Winners Dog and Reserve Winners Bitch are also awarded but do not carry any points unless the Winners win is disallowed by AKC. The Winners Dog and Bitch compete with the specials (those dogs that have attained championship) for Best of Breed or Variety, Best of Winners and Best of Opposite Sex. It is possible to pick up an extra point or even a major if the points are higher for the defeated winner than those of Best of Winners. The latter would get the higher total from the defeated winner.

At an all-breed show, each Best of Breed or Variety winner will go on to his respective Group and then the Group winners will compete against each other for Best in Show. There are seven Groups: Sporting, Hounds, Working, Terriers, Toys, Non-Sporting and Herding. Obviously there are no Groups at speciality shows (those shows that have only one breed or a show such as the American Spaniel Club's Flushing Spaniel Show, which is for all flushing spaniel breeds).

Westminster Kennel Club is our most prestigious show although the entry is limited to 2500. In recent years, entry has been limited to Champions. This show is more formal than the majority of the shows with the judges wearing formal attire and the handlers fashionably dressed. In most instances the quality of the dogs is superb. After all, it is a show of Champions. It is a good show to study the AKC registered breeds and is by far the most exciting–especially since it is televised! WKC is one of the few shows in this country that is still benched. This means the dog must be in his benched area during the show hours except when he is being groomed, in the ring, or being exercised.

These Australian Shepherds are in position in the show ring to be judged. Each handler is responsible for his or her dog's actions in the ring.

In England, Crufts is The Kennel Club's own show and is most assuredly the largest dog show in the world. They've been known to have an entry of nearly 20,000, and the show lasts four days. Entry is only gained by qualifying through winning in specified classes at another Championship Show. Westminster is strictly conformation, but Crufts exhibitors and spectators enjoy not only conformation but obedience, agility and a multitude of exhibitions as well. Obedience was admitted in 1957 and agility in 1983.

The Westminster Kennel Club Dog Show is the most prestigious in the United States. It is held in New York City every February.

Bring all the necessities with you to the dog show. An exercise pen is used to keep your Aussies safe and secure between events.

Junior Showmanship

The Junior Showmanship Class is a wonderful way to build self confidence even if there are no aspirations of staying with the dog-show game later in life. Frequently,

Junior Showmanship becomes the background of those who become successful exhibitors/handlers in the future. In some instances it is taken very seriously, and success is measured in terms of wins. The Junior Handler is judged solely on his ability and skill in presenting his dog. The dog's conformation is not to be considered by the judge. Even so the condition and grooming of the dog may be a reflection upon the handler.

Usually the matches and point shows include different classes. The Junior Handler's dog may be entered in a breed or obedience class and even shown by another person in that class. Junior Showmanship classes are usually divided by age and perhaps sex. The age is determined by the handler's age on the day of the show. The classes are:

Novice Junior for those at least ten and under 14 years of age who at time of entry closing have not won three first places in a Novice Class at a licensed or member show.

Novice Senior for those at least 14 and under 18 years of age who at the time of entry closing have not won three first places in a Novice Class at a licensed or member show.

Open Junior for those at least ten and under 14 years of age who at the time of entry closing have won at least three first places in a Novice Junior Showmanship Class at a licensed or member show with competition present.

Open Senior for those at least 14 and under 18 years of age who at time of entry closing have won at least three first places in a Novice Junior Showmanship Class at a licensed or member show with competition present.

Junior Handlers must include their AKC Junior Handler number on each show entry. This needs to be obtained from the AKC.

Your Australian Shepherd can compete for the AKC sponsored Canine Good Citizen Certificate, designed to encourage owners to properly train their dogs.

CANINE GOOD CITIZEN

The AKC sponsors a program to encourage dog

Excellent grooming is important in the show ring, but its important for a healthy pet, too, which is why it's part of the Canine Good Citizen Test.

owners to train their dogs. Local clubs perform the pass/fail tests, and dogs who pass are awarded a Canine Good Citizen Certificate. Proof of vaccination is required at the time of participation. The test includes:

1. Accepting a friendly stranger.
2. Sitting politely for petting.
3. Appearance and grooming.
4. Walking on a loose leash.
5. Walking through a crowd.
6. Sit and down on command/staying in place.
7. Come when called.
8. Reaction to another dog.
9. Reactions to distractions.
10. Supervised separation.

If more effort was made by pet owners to accomplish these exercises, fewer dogs would be cast off to the humane shelter.

Obedience

Obedience is necessary, without a doubt, but it can also become a wonderful hobby or even an obsession. In my opinion, obedience classes and competition can provide wonderful companionship, not only with your dog but with your classmates or fellow competitors. It is always gratifying to discuss your dog's problems with others who have had similar experiences. The AKC acknowledged Obedience around 1936, and it has changed tremendously even though many of the exercises are basically the same. Today, obedience competition is just that–very competitive. Even so, it is possible for every obedience exhibitor to come home a winner (by earning qualifying scores) even though he/she may not earn a placement in the class.

This Australian Shepherd bred by Margaret Cameron and Jo Kimes and owned by Carol Ann Hartnagle-Madsen is a shining example of the breed.

Most of the obedience titles are awarded after earning three qualifying scores (legs) in the appropriate class under three different judges. These classes offer a perfect score of 200, which is extremely rare. Each of the class exercises has its own point value. A leg is earned after receiving a score of at least 170 and at least 50 percent of the points available in each exercise. The titles are:

Companion Dog–CD

This is called the Novice Class and the exercises are:

1. Heel on leash and figure 8	40 points
2. Stand for examination	30 points
3. Heel free	40 points
4. Recall	30 points
5. Long sit–one minute	30 points
6. Long down–three minutes	30 points
Maximum total score	200 points

Companion Dog Excellent–CDX

This is the Open Class and the exercises are:

1. Heel off leash and figure 8	40 points
2. Drop on recall	30 points
3. Retrieve on flat	20 points
4. Retrieve over high jump	30 points
5. Broad jump	20 points
6. Long sit–three minutes (out of sight)	30 points
7. Long down–five minutes (out of sight)	30 points
Maximum total score	200 points

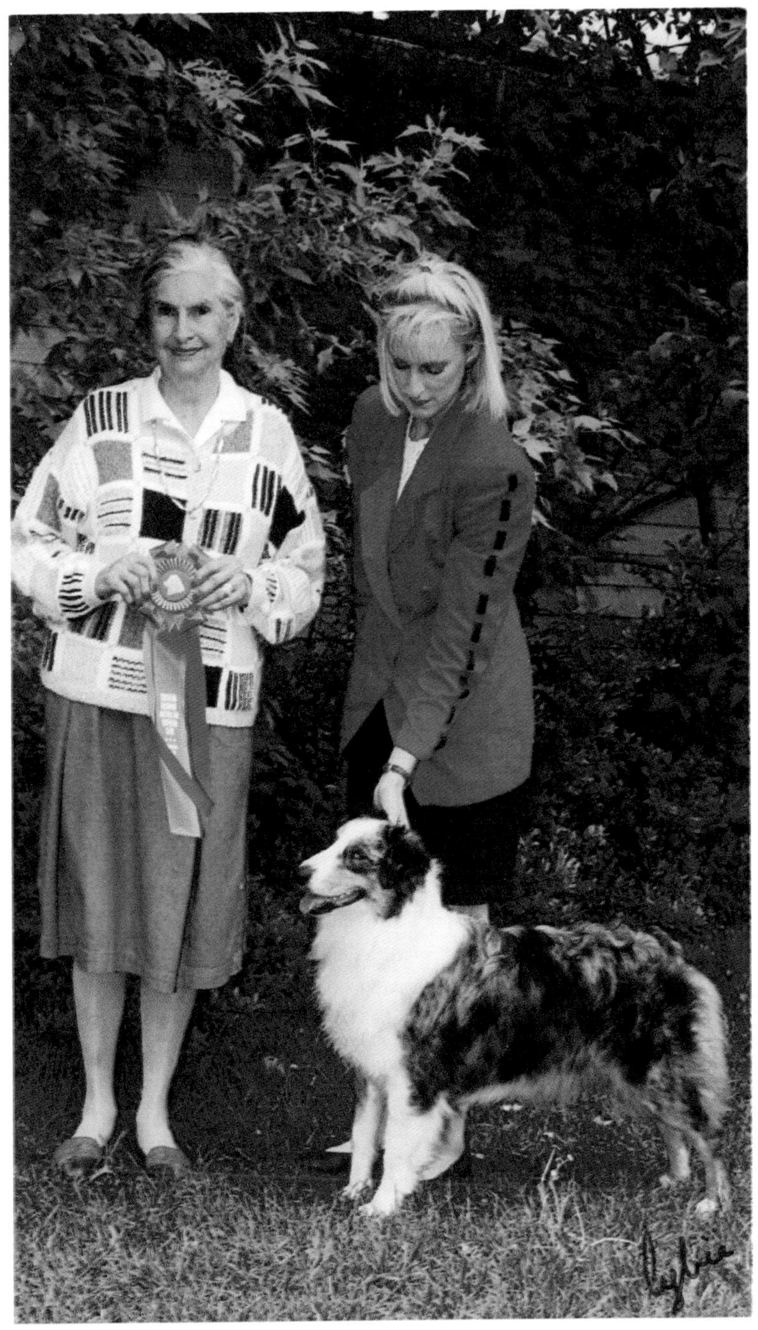

Utility Dog–UD

The Utility Class exercises are:

1. Signal Exercise	40 points
2. Scent discrimination-Article 1	30 points
3. Scent discrimination-Article 2	30 points
4. Directed retrieve	30 points
5. Moving stand and examination	30 points
6. Directed jumping	40 points
Maximum total score	200 points

After achieving the UD title, you may feel inclined to go after the UDX and/or OTCh. The UDX (Utility Dog Excellent) title went into effect in January 1994. It is not easily attained. The title requires qualifying simultaneously ten times in Open B and Utility B but not necessarily at consecutive shows.

The OTCh (Obedience Trial Champion) is awarded after the dog has earned his UD and then goes on to earn 100 championship points, a first place in Utility, a first place in Open and another first place in either class. The placements must be won under three different judges at all-breed obedience trials. The points are determined by the number of dogs competing in the Open B and Utility B classes. The OTCh title precedes the dog's name.

Obedience matches (AKC Sanctioned, Fun, and Show and Go) are usually available. Usually they are sponsored by the local obedience clubs. When preparing an obedience dog for a title, you will find matches very helpful. Fun Matches and Show and Go Matches are more lenient in allowing you to make corrections in the ring. I frequently train (correct) in the ring and inform the judge that I would like to do so and to please mark me "exhibition." This means that I will not be eligible for any prize. This type of training is usually very necessary for the Open and Utility Classes. AKC Sanctioned Obedience Matches do not allow corrections in the ring since they must abide by the AKC Obedience Regulations. If you are interested in showing in obedience, then you should contact the AKC for a copy of the Obedience Regulations.

TRACKING

Tracking is officially classified obedience, but I feel it should have its own category. There are three tracking titles available:

Tracking Dog (TD), Tracking Dog Excellent (TDX), Variable Surface Tracking (VST). If all three tracking titles are obtained, then the dog officially becomes a CT (Champion Tracker). The CT will go in front of the dog's name.

A TD may be earned anytime and does not have to follow the other obedience titles. There are many exhibitors that prefer tracking to obedience, and there are others like myself that do both. In my experience with small dogs, I prefer to earn the CD and CDX before attempting tracking. My reasoning is that small dogs are closer to the mat in the obedience rings and therefore it's too easy to put the nose down and sniff. Tracking encourages sniffing. Of course this depends on the dog. I've had some dogs that tracked around the ring and others (TDXs) who wouldn't think of sniffing in the ring.

Training to compete is not an easy task, but the satisfaction you'll receive when you accomplish your goals is rewarding for both you and your Aussie.

Tracking Dog–TD

A dog must be certified by an AKC tracking judge that he is ready to perform in an AKC test. The AKC can provide the names of tracking judges in your area that you can contact for certification. Depending on where you live, you may have to travel a distance if there is no local tracking judge. The certification track will be equivalent to a regular AKC track. A regulation track must be 440 to 500 yards long with at least two right-angle turns out in the open. The track will be aged 30 minutes to two hours. The handler has two starting flags at the beginning of the track to indicate the direction started. The dog works on a harness and 40-foot lead and must work at least 20 feet in front of the handler. An article (either a dark glove or wallet) will be dropped at the end of the track, and the dog must indicate it but not necessarily retrieve it.

This beautiful Australian Shepherd is Ch. Los Pinos Rolling Thunder, a blue merle owned by Judith Frey.

People always ask me what the dog tracks. In my opinion, initially, the beginner on the short-aged track tracks the tracklayer. Eventually the dog learns to track the disturbed vegetation and learns to differentiate between tracks. Getting started with tracking requires reading the AKC regulations and a good book on tracking plus finding other tracking enthusiasts. I like to work on the buddy system. That is–we lay tracks for each other so we can practice blind tracks. It is possible to train on your own, but if you are a beginner, it is a lot more entertaining to track with a buddy. Tracking is my favorite dog sport. It's rewarding seeing the dog use his natural ability.

Tracking Dog Excellent–TDX

Obedience training allows the Australian Shepherd and his owner to develop a closeness formed from working together.

The TDX track is 800 to 1000 yards long and is aged three to five hours. There will be five to seven turns. An article is left at the starting flag, and three other articles must be indicated on the track. There is only one flag at the start, so it is a blind start. Approximately one and a half hours after the track is laid, two tracklayers will cross over the track at two different places to test the dog's ability to stay with the original track. There will be at least two obstacles on the track such as a change of cover, fences, creeks, ditches, etc. The dog must have a TD before entering a TDX. There is no certification required for a TDX.

Variable Surface Tracking–VST

This test came into effect September 1995. The dog must have a TD earned at least six months prior to entering this test. The track is 600 to 800 yards long and shall have a minimum of three different surfaces. Vegetation shall be included along with two areas devoid of vegetation such as concrete, asphalt, gravel, sand, hard pan or mulch. The areas devoid of vegetation shall comprise at least one-third to one-half of the track. The track is aged three to five hours. There will be four to eight turns and four numbered articles including one leather, one plastic, one metal and one fabric dropped on the track. There is one starting flag. The handler will work at least 10 feet from the dog.

Agility competitions test a dog's coordination. Here, Doomer's giving the teeter-totter a try. Owner, Kelly Kemp.

Agility is an action-packed sport that is as exciting for the handler and spectators as it is for the dogs.

AGILITY

Agility was first introduced by John Varley in England at the Crufts Dog Show, February 1978, but Peter Meanwell, competitor and judge, actually developed the idea. It was officially recognized in the early '80s. Agility is extremely popular in England and Canada and growing in popularity in the U.S. The AKC acknowledged agility in August 1994. Dogs must be at least 12 months of age to be entered. It is a fascinating sport that the dog, handler and spectators enjoy to the utmost. Agility is a spectator sport! The dog performs off lead. The handler either runs with his dog or positions himself on the course and directs his dog with verbal and hand signals over a timed course over or through a variety of obstacles including a time out or pause. One of the main drawbacks to agility is finding a place to train. The obstacles take up a lot of space and it is very time consuming to put up and take down courses.

The titles earned at AKC agility trials are Novice Agility Dog (NAD), Open Agility Dog (OAD), Agility Dog Excellent (ADX), and Master Agility Excellent (MAX). In order to acquire an agility title, a dog must earn a qualifying score in its respective class on three separate occasions under two different judges. The MAX will be awarded after earning ten qualifying scores in the Agility Excellent Class.

Performance Tests

During the last decade the American Kennel Club has promoted performance tests—those events that test the different breeds' natural abilities. This type of event encourages a handler to devote even more time to his dog and retain the natural instincts of his breed heritage. It is an important part of the wonderful world of dogs.

Lure Coursing

For all sighthounds (Afghans, Basenjis, Borzois, Greyhounds, Ibizans, Irish Wolfhounds, Pharaoh Hounds, Rhodesian

This is Ch. Las Rocosa Alice Blue with Carol Ann Hartnagle-Madsen.

Ridgebacks, Salukis, Scottish Deerhounds, and Whippets).

The participant must be at least one year of age, and dogs with limited registration (ILP) are elgible. They chase a lure of three plastic bags and are judged on overall ability, follow, speed, agility and endurance. Like the other AKC performance tests, lure coursing gives dogs the opportunity to prove themselves at what they were originally bred to do.

Junior Courser (JC) A hound running alone shall receive certification from a judge on one date, and a second certification at a later time, stating the hound completed a 600-yard course with a minimum of four turns. The hound must complete the course with enthusiasm and without interruption.

Senior Courser (SC) Must be elgible to enter the open stake and the hound must run with at least one other hound. Must receive qualifying scores at four AKC-licensed or member trials under two different judges.

Field Championship (FC) Prefix to the hound's name. Must receive 15 championship points including two first placements with three points or more under two different judges.

Herding competitions are a great place for your Australian Shepherd to show off his considerable skills and be recognized for his contribution to ranching.

Earthdog Events

For small terriers (Australian, Bedlington, Border, Cairn, Dandie Dinmont, Fox (Smooth & Wire), Lakeland, Norfolk, Norwich, Scottish, Sealyham, Skye, Welsh, West Highland White and Dachshunds).

Limited registration (ILP) dogs are eligible and all entrants must be at least six months of age. The primary purpose of the small terriers and Dachshunds is to pursue quarry to ground, hold the game, and alert the hunter where to dig, or to bolt. There are two parts to the test: (1) the approach to the quarry and (2) working the quarry. The dog must pass both parts for a Junior Earthdog (JE). The Senior Earthdog (SE) must do a third part–to leave the den on command. The Master Earthdog (ME) is a bit more complicated.

Hunting Titles

For retrievers, pointing breeds and spaniels. Titles offered are Junior Hunter (JH), Senior Hunter (SH), and Master Hunter (MH).

Flushing Spaniels Their primary purpose is to hunt, find, flush and return birds to hand as quickly as possible in a pleasing and obedient manner. The entrant must be at least six months of age and dogs with limited registration (ILP) are eligible. Game used are pigeons, pheasants, and quail.

Retrievers Limited registration (ILP) retrievers are not eligible to compete in Hunting Tests. The purpose of a Hunting Test for retrievers is to test the merits of and evaluate the abilities of retrievers in the field in order to determine their suitability and ability as hunting companions. They are expected to retrieve any type of game bird, pheasants, ducks, pigeons, guinea hens and quail.

Pointing Breeds Are eligible at six months of age, and dogs with limited registration (ILP) are permitted. They must show a keen desire to hunt; be bold and independent; have a fast, yet attractive, manner of hunting; and demonstrate intelligence not only in seeking objectives but also in the ability to find game. They must establish point, and in the more advanced tests they need to be steady to wing and must remain in position until the bird is shot or they are released.

A Senior Hunter must retrieve. A Master Hunter must honor. The judges and the marshal are permitted to ride horseback during the test, but all handling must be done on foot.

Herding Titles

For all Herding breeds and Rottweilers and Samoyeds. Entrants must be at least nine months of age and dogs with limited registration (ILP) are eligible. The Herding

The herding program is divided into two sections, testing and trial, and the goal is to demonstrate proficiency in herding different types of livestock in different situations.

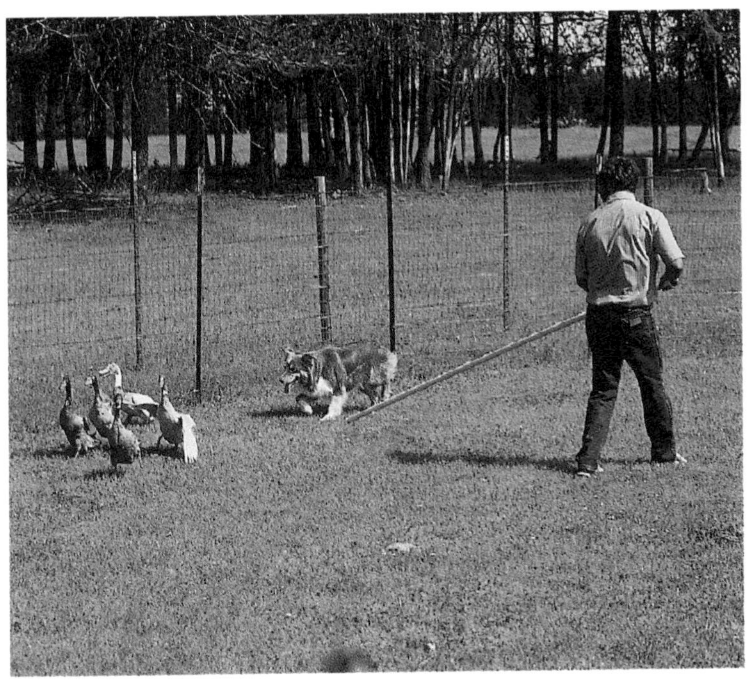

This red Australian Shepherd is performing in a herding instinct test.

program is divided into Testing and Trial sections. The goal is to demonstrate proficiency in herding livestock in diverse situations. The titles offered are Herding Started (HS), Herding Intermediate (HI), and Herding Excellent (HX). Upon completion of the HX a Herding Championship may be earned after accumulating 15 championship points.

The above information has been taken from the AKC Guidelines for the appropriate events.

SCHUTZHUND

The German word "Schutzhund" translated to English means "Protection Dog." It is a fast growing competitive sport in the United States and has been popular in England since the early 1900s. Schutzhund was originally a test to determine which German Shepherds were quality dogs for breeding in Germany. It gives us the ability to test our dogs for correct temperament and working ability. Like every other dog sport, it requires teamwork between the handler and the dog.

Schutzhund training and showing involves three phases: Tracking, Obedience and Protection. There are three SchH levels: SchH I (novice), SchH II (intermediate), and SchH III (advanced). Each title becomes progressively more difficult. The handler and dog start out in each phase with 100 points. Points are deducted as errors are incurred. A total perfect score is 300, and for a dog and handler to earn a title he must earn at least 70 points in tracking and obedience and at least 80 points in protection. Today many different breeds participate successfully in Schutzhund.

GENERAL INFORMATION

Obedience, tracking and agility allow the purebred dog with an Indefinite Listing Privilege (ILP) number or a limited registration to be exhibited and earn titles. Application must be made to the AKC for an ILP number.

The American Kennel Club publishes a monthly *Events* magazine that is part of the *Gazette*, their official journal for the sport of purebred dogs. The *Events* section lists upcoming shows and the secretary or superintendent for them. The majority of the conformation shows in the U.S. are overseen by licensed superintendents. Generally the entry closing date is approximately two-and-a-half weeks before the actual show. Point shows are fairly expensive, while the match shows cost about one third of the point show entry fee. Match shows usually take entries the day of the show but some are pre-entry. The best way to find match show information is through your local kennel club. Upon asking, the AKC can provide you with a list of superintendents, and you can write and ask to be put on their mailing lists.

This is Hall of Fame Sire Ch. Las Rocosa Little Wolf with Jeanne Joy Hartnagle-Taylor.

Obedience trial and tracking test information is available through the AKC. Frequently these events are not superintended, but put on by the host club. Therefore you would make the entry with the event's secretary.

As you have read, there are numerous activities you can share with your dog. Regardless what you do, it does take teamwork. Your dog can only benefit from your attention and training. I hope this chapter has enlightened you and hope, if nothing else, you will attend a show here and there. Perhaps you will start with a puppy kindergarten class, and who knows where it may lead!

Even if you never enter a show, the attention and training you give to your Australian Shepherd puppy can only benefit both of you in the long run. Owner, Lucinda Howard.

This is the Las Rocosa gang of Boulder, Colorado, the ASCA's number one Hall of Fame Australian Shepherd breeders.

HEALTH CARE for the Australian Shepherd

Veterinary medicine has become far more sophisticated than what was available to our ancestors. This can be attributed to the increase in household pets and consequently the demand for better care for them. Also human medicine has become far more complex. Today diagnostic testing in veterinary medicine parallels human diagnostics. Because of better technology we can expect our pets to live healthier lives thereby increasing their life spans.

Puppies are very vulnerable and need to see a veterinarian as soon as possible after you acquire them. These four-week-old Aussies are owned by David and Vicky Whipp.

THE FIRST CHECK UP

You will want to take your new puppy/dog in for its first check up within 48 to 72 hours after acquiring it. Many breeders strongly recommend this check up and so do the humane shelters. A puppy/dog can appear healthy but it may have a serious problem that is not apparent to the layman. Most pets have some type of a minor flaw that may never cause a real problem.

Unfortunately if he/she should have a serious problem, you will want to consider the consequences of keeping the pet and the attachments that will be formed, which may be broken prematurely. Keep in mind there are many healthy dogs looking for good homes.

This first check up is a good time to establish yourself with

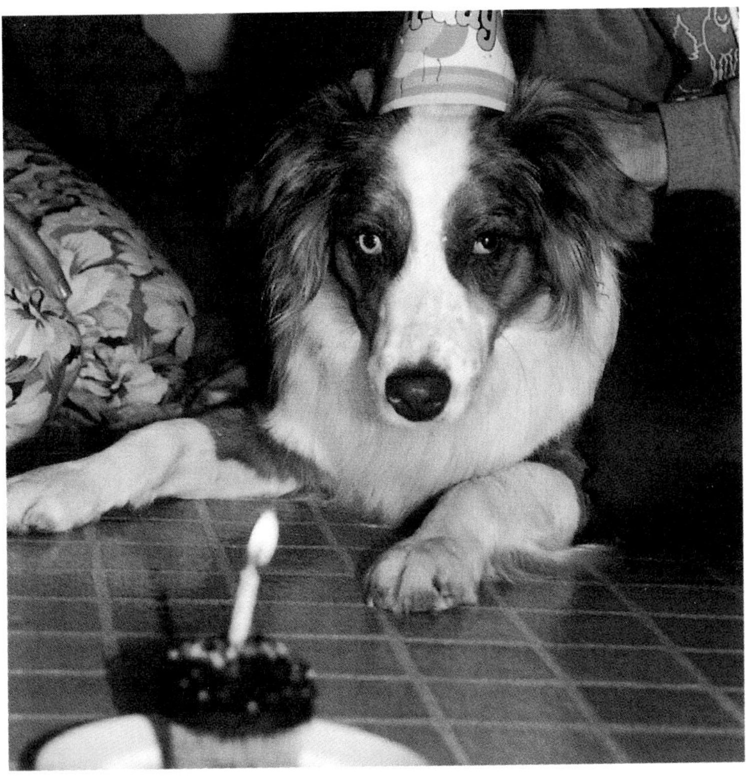

Your Aussie should receive all his necessary immunizations early in life to be assured of a healthy first year. Your pet's first birthday party should be a happy, healthy one!

the veterinarian and learn the office policy regarding their hours and how they handle emergencies. Usually the breeder or another conscientious pet owner is a good reference for locating a capable veterinarian. You should be aware that not all veterinarians give the same quality of service. Please do not make your selection on the least expensive clinic, as they may be short changing your pet. There is the possibility that eventually it will cost you more due to improper diagnosis, treatment, etc. If you are selecting a new veterinarian, feel free to ask for a tour of the clinic. You should inquire about making an appointment for a tour since all clinics are working clinics, and therefore may not be available all day for sightseers. You may worry less if you see where your pet will be spending the day if he ever needs to be hospitalized.

THE PHYSICAL EXAM

Your veterinarian will check your pet's overall condition, which includes listening to the heart; checking the respiration; feeling the abdomen, muscles and joints; checking the mouth, which includes the gum color and signs of gum disease along with plaque buildup; checking the ears for signs of an infection or ear mites; examining the eyes; and, last but not least, checking the condition of the skin and coat.

He should ask you questions regarding your pet's eating and elimination habits and invite you to relay your questions. It is a good idea to prepare a list so as not to forget anything. He should discuss the proper diet and the quantity to be fed. If this should differ from your breeder's recommendation, then you should convey to him the breeder's choice and see if he approves. If he recommends changing the diet, then this should be done over a few days so as not to cause a gastrointestinal upset. It is customary to take in a fresh stool sample (just a small amount) for a test for intestinal parasites. It must be fresh, preferably within 12 hours, since the eggs hatch quickly and after hatching will not be observed under the microscope. If your pet isn't obliging then, usually the technician can take one in the clinic.

IMMUNIZATIONS

It is important that you take your puppy/dog's vaccination record with you on your first visit. In case of a puppy, presumably the breeder has seen to the vaccinations up to the

Maternal antibodies protect puppies from disease the first few weeks of life. Vaccinations are needed because the antibodies are only temporarily effective.

time you acquired custody. Veterinarians differ in their vaccination protocol. It is not unusual for your puppy to have received vaccinations for distemper, hepatitis, leptospirosis, parvovirus and parainfluenza every two to three weeks from the age of five or six weeks. Usually this is a combined injection and is typically called the DHLPP. The DHLPP is given through at least 12 to 14 weeks of age, and it is customary to continue with another parvovirus vaccine at 16 to 18 weeks. You may wonder why so many immunizations are necessary. No one knows for sure when the puppy's maternal antibodies are gone, although it is customarily accepted that distemper antibodies are gone by 12 weeks. Usually parvovirus antibodies are gone by 16 to 18 weeks of age. However, it is possible for the maternal antibodies to be gone at a much earlier age or even a later age. Therefore immunizations are started at an early age. The vaccine will not give immunity as long as there are maternal antibodies.

Internal parasites can be passed from dam to puppy, so assume that all puppies have worms and treat them as such.

The rabies vaccination is given at three or six months of age depending on your local laws. A vaccine for bordetella (kennel cough) is advisable and can be given anytime from the age of five weeks. The coronavirus is not commonly given unless there is a problem locally. The Lyme vaccine is necessary in endemic areas. Lyme disease has been reported in 47 states.

Distemper

This is virtually an incurable disease. If the dog recovers, he is subject to severe nervous disorders. The virus attacks every tissue in the body and resembles a bad cold with a fever. It can cause a runny nose and eyes and cause gastrointestinal disorders, including a poor appetite, vomiting and diarrhea. The virus is carried by raccoons, foxes, wolves, mink and other dogs. Unvaccinated youngsters and senior citizens are very susceptible. This is still a common disease.

Hepatitis

This is a virus that is most serious in very young dogs. It is spread by contact with an infected animal or its stool or urine. The virus affects the liver and kidneys and is characterized by high fever, depression and lack of appetite. Recovered animals may be afflicted with chronic illnesses.

Leptospirosis

This is a bacterial disease transmitted by contact with the urine of an infected dog, rat or other wildlife. It produces severe symptoms of fever, depression, jaundice and internal bleeding and was fatal before the vaccine was developed. Recovered dogs can be carriers, and the disease can be transmitted from dogs to humans.

Parvovirus

This was first noted in the late 1970s and is still a fatal disease. However, with proper vaccinations, early diagnosis and prompt treatment, it is a manageable disease. It attacks the bone marrow and intestinal tract. The symptoms include depression, loss of appetite, vomiting, diarrhea and collapse. Immediate medical attention is of the essence.

Rabies

This is shed in the saliva and is carried by raccoons, skunks, foxes, other dogs and cats. It attacks nerve tissue, resulting in paralysis and death. Rabies can be transmitted to people and is

Bordetella attached to canine cilia. Otherwise known as kennel cough, this disease is highly contagious and should be vaccinated against routinely.

virtually always fatal. This disease is reappearing in the suburbs.

Bordetella (Kennel Cough)

The symptoms are coughing, sneezing, hacking and retching accompanied by nasal discharge usually lasting from a few days to several weeks. There are several disease-producing organisms responsible for this disease. The present vaccines are helpful but do not protect for all the strains. It usually is not life threatening but in some instances it can progress to a serious bronchopneumonia. The disease is highly contagious. The vaccination should be given routinely for dogs that come in contact with other dogs, such as through boarding, training class or visits to the groomer.

The deer tick is the most common carrier of Lyme disease. Photo courtesy of Virbac Laboratories, Inc., Fort Worth, Texas.

Coronavirus

This is usually self limiting and not

Dogs can pick up diseases from other dogs, so make sure your Aussie is properly vaccinated before taking him out to make friends.

life threatening. It was first noted in the late '70s about a year before parvovirus. The virus produces a yellow/brown stool and there may be depression, vomiting and diarrhea.

Lyme Disease

This was first diagnosed in the United States in 1976 in Lyme, CT in people who lived in close proximity to the deer tick. Symptoms may include acute lameness, fever, swelling of joints and loss of appetite. Your veterinarian can advise you if you live in an endemic area.

After your puppy has completed his puppy vaccinations, you will continue to booster the DHLPP once a year. It is customary to booster the rabies one year after the first vaccine and then, depending on where you live, it should be boostered every year or every three years. This depends on your local laws. The Lyme and corona vaccines are boostered annually and it is recommended that the bordetella be boostered every six to eight months.

ANNUAL VISIT

I would like to impress the importance of the annual check up, which would include the booster vaccinations, check for intestinal

Hookworms are almost microscopic intestinal worms that can cause anemia and therefore serious problems, even death.

parasites and test for heartworm. Today in our very busy world it is rush, rush and see "how much you can get for how little." Unbelievably, some non-veterinary businesses have entered into the vaccination business. More harm than good can come to your dog through improper vaccinations, possibly from inferior vaccines and/or the wrong schedule. More than likely you truly care about your companion dog and over the years you have devoted much time and expense to his well being. Perhaps you are unaware that a vaccination is not just a vaccination. There is more involved. Please, please follow through with regular physical examinations. It is so important for your veterinarian to know your dog and this is especially true during middle age through the geriatric years. More than likely your older dog will require more than one physical a year. The annual physical is good preventive medicine. Through early diagnosis and subsequent treatment your dog can maintain a longer and better quality of life.

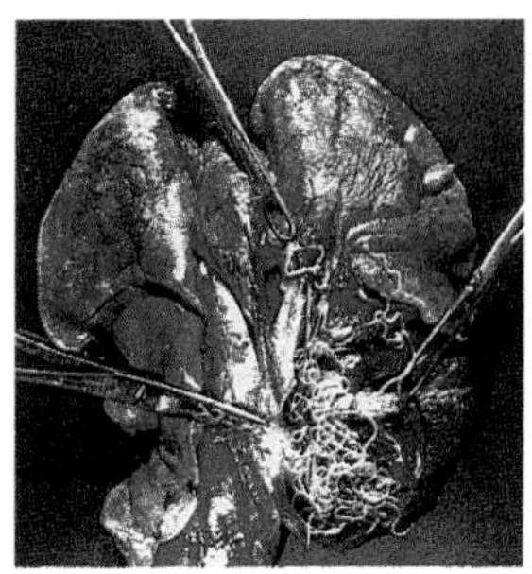

Dirofilaria - adult worms in a heart of a dog. Courtesy of Merck Ag Vet.

Intestinal Parasites

Hookworms

These are almost microscopic intestinal worms that can cause anemia and therefore serious problems, including death, in young puppies. Hookworms can be transmitted to humans through penetration of the skin. Puppies may be born with them.

Roundworms

These are spaghetti-like worms that can cause a potbellied appearance and dull coat along with more severe symptoms, such as vomiting, diarrhea and coughing. Puppies acquire these while in the mother's uterus and through lactation. Both hookworms and roundworms may be acquired through ingestion.

The more time your Australian Shepherd spends outside the more chance he has of picking up parasites. Make sure to check your Aussie's coat often for fleas and ticks.

Whipworms

These have a three-month life cycle and are not acquired through the dam. They cause intermittent diarrhea usually with mucus. Whipworms are possibly the most difficult worm to eradicate. Their eggs are very resistant to most environmental factors and can last for years until the proper conditions enable them to mature. Whipworms are seldom seen in the stool.

Intestinal parasites are more prevalent in some areas than others. Climate, soil and contamination are big factors contributing to the incidence of intestinal parasites. Eggs are passed in the stool, lay on the ground and then become infective in a certain number of days. Each of the above worms has a different life cycle. Your best chance of becoming and remaining worm-free is to always pooper-scoop your yard. A fenced-in yard keeps stray dogs out, which is certainly helpful.

I would recommend having a fecal examination on your dog twice a year or more often if there is a problem. If your dog has a positive fecal sample, then he will be given the appropriate medication and you will be asked to bring back another stool sample in a certain period of time (depending on the type of worm) and then be rewormed. This process goes on until he has at least two negative samples. The different types of worms require different medications. You will be wasting your money and doing your dog an injustice by buying over-the-counter medication without first consulting your veterinarian.

Other Internal Parasites

Coccidiosis and Giardiasis

These protozoal infections usually affect puppies, especially in places where large numbers of puppies are brought together. Older dogs may harbor these infections but do not show signs unless they are stressed. Symptoms include diarrhea, weight loss and lack of appetite. These infections are not always apparent in the fecal examination.

Whipworms are hard to find without a microscope and this is best left for the veterinarian. Pictured here are adult whipworms.

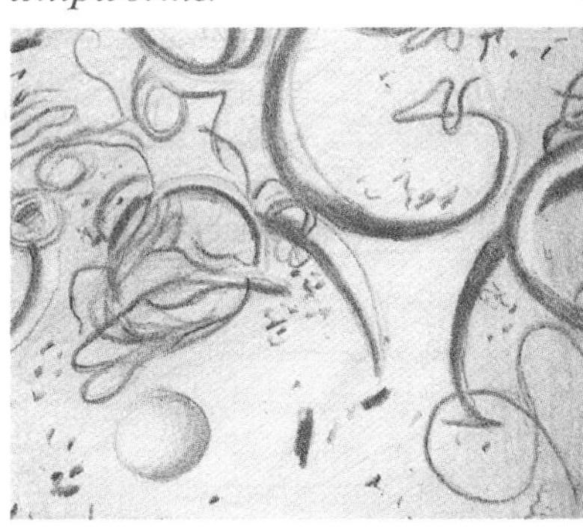

Tapeworms

Seldom apparent on fecal floatation, they are diagnosed frequently as rice-like segments around the dog's anus and the base of the tail. Tapeworms are long, flat and ribbon like, sometimes several feet in length, and made up of many segments about five-eighths of an inch long. The two most common types of tapeworms found in the dog are:

(1) First the larval form of the flea tapeworm parasite must mature in an intermediate host, the flea, before it can

become infective. Your dog acquires this by ingesting the flea through licking and chewing.

(2) Rabbits, rodents and certain large game animals serve as intermediate hosts for other species of tapeworms. If your dog should eat one of these infected hosts, then he can acquire tapeworms.

HEARTWORM DISEASE

This is a worm that resides in the heart and adjacent blood vessels of the lung that produces microfilaria, which circulate in the bloodstream. It is possible for a dog to be infected with any number of worms from one to a hundred that can be 6 to 14 inches long. It is a life-threatening disease, expensive to treat and easily prevented. Depending on where you live, your veterinarian may recommend a preventive year-round and either an annual or semiannual blood test. The most common preventive is given once a month.

EXTERNAL PARASITES

Fleas

These pests are not only the dog's worst enemy but also enemy to the owner's pocketbook. Preventing is less expensive than treating, but regardless I think we'd prefer to spend our money elsewhere. I would guess that the majority of our dogs are allergic to the bite of a flea, and in many cases it only takes one flea bite. The protein in the flea's saliva is the culprit. Allergic dogs have a reaction, which usually results in a "hot spot." More than likely such a reaction will involve a trip to the veterinarian for treatment. Yes, prevention is less expensive. Fortunately today there are several good products available.

If there is a flea infestation, no one product is going to correct the problem. Not only will the dog require treatment so will the environment. In general flea collars are not very effective although there is now available an "egg" collar that will kill the eggs on the dog. Dips are the most economical but they are messy. There are some effective shampoos and treatments available through pet shops and veterinarians. An oral tablet arrived on the American market in 1995 and was popular in Europe the previous year. It sterilizes the female flea but will not kill adult fleas. Therefore the tablet, which is given monthly, will decrease the flea population but is not a "cure-all." Those dogs that suffer from flea-bite allergy will still be subjected to the bite of the flea. Another popular parasiticide is permethrin, which is applied to the back of the dog in one or two places depending on the dog's weight. This product works as a repellent causing the flea to get "hot feet" and jump off. Do not confuse this product with some of the organophosphates that are also applied to the dog's back.

Some products are not usable on young puppies. Treating fleas should be done under your veterinarian's guidance. Frequently it is necessary to combine products and the layman does not have the knowledge regarding possible toxicities. It is hard to believe but there are a few dogs that do have a natural resistance to fleas. Nevertheless it would be wise to treat all pets at the same time. Don't forget your cats. Cats just love to prowl the neighborhood and consequently return with unwanted guests.

Heartworm is a life-threatening disease that can be detected through blood tests. Depending on where you live, your veterinarian may recommend preventive treatment.

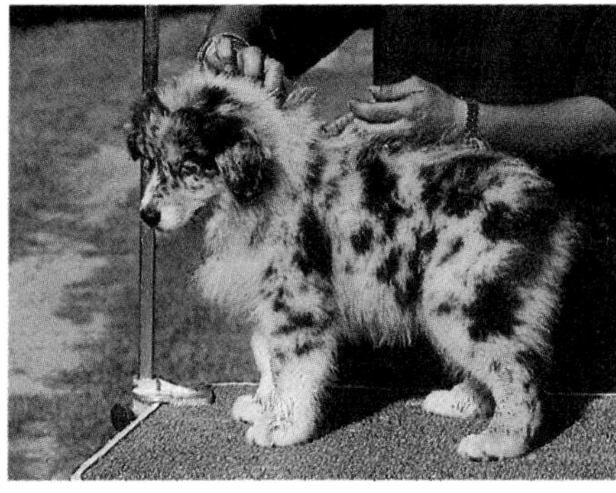

Adult fleas live on the dog but their eggs drop off the dog into the environment. There they go through four larval stages before reaching adulthood, and thereby are able to jump back on the poor unsuspecting dog. The cycle resumes and takes between 21 to 28 days under ideal conditions. There are environmental products available that will kill both the adult fleas and the larvae.

Ticks

Ticks carry Rocky Mountain Spotted Fever, Lyme disease and can cause tick paralysis. They should be removed with tweezers, trying to pull out the head. The jaws carry disease.

There is a tick preventive collar that does an excellent job. The ticks automatically back out on those dogs wearing collars.

Sarcoptic Mange

This is a mite that is difficult to find on skin scrapings. The pinnal reflex is a good indicator of this disease. Rub the ends of the pinna (ear) together and the dog will start scratching with his foot. Sarcoptes are highly contagious to other dogs and to humans although they do not live long on humans. They cause intense itching.

Demodectic Mange

This is a mite that is passed from the dam to her puppies. It affects youngsters age three to ten months. Diagnosis is confirmed by skin scraping. Small areas of alopecia around the eyes, lips and/or forelegs become visible. There is little itching unless there is a secondary bacterial infection. Some breeds are afflicted more than others.

Cheyletiella

This causes intense itching and is diagnosed by skin scraping. It lives in the outer layers of the skin of dogs,

A flea collar is a good start to prevent external parasites, but a regular, careful grooming regimen is the best way to nip any infestations in the bud.

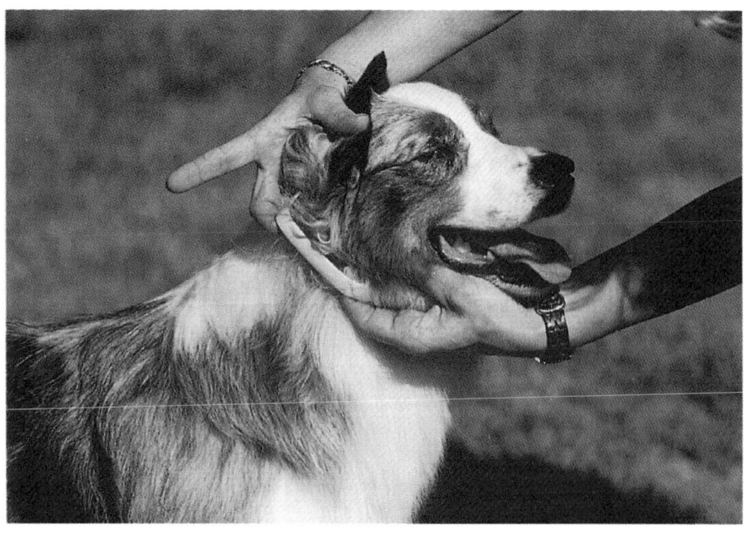

Outdoor areas can be highly infested with fleas and ticks. Be sure to inspect your Australian Shepherd after an outdoor romp.

cats, rabbits and humans. Yellow-gray scales may be found on the back and the rump, top of the head and the nose.

To Breed or Not To Breed

More than likely your breeder has requested that you have your puppy neutered or spayed. Your breeder's request is based on what is healthiest for your dog and what is most beneficial for your breed. Experienced and conscientious breeders devote many years into developing a bloodline. In order to do this, he makes every effort to plan each breeding in regard to conformation, temperament and health. This type of breeder does his best to perform the necessary testing (i.e., OFA, CERF, testing for inherited blood disorders, thyroid, etc.). Testing is expensive and sometimes very disheartening when a favorite dog doesn't pass his health tests. The health history pertains not only to the breeding stock but to the immediate ancestors. Reputable breeders do not want their offspring to be bred indiscriminately. Therefore you may be asked to neuter or spay your puppy. Of course there is always the exception, and your breeder may agree to let you breed your dog under his direct supervision. This is an important concept. More and more effort is being made to breed healthier dogs.

Spay/Neuter

There are numerous benefits of performing this surgery at six months of age. Unspayed females are subject to mammary and ovarian cancer. In order to prevent mammary cancer she must be spayed prior to her first heat cycle. Later in life, an unspayed female may develop a pyometra (an infected uterus), which is definitely life threatening.

Spaying is performed under a general anesthetic and is easy on the young dog. As you might expect it is a little harder on the older dog, but that is no reason to deny her the surgery. The surgery removes the ovaries and uterus. It is important to remove all the ovarian tissue. If some is left behind, she could remain attractive to males. In order to view the ovaries, a reasonably long incision is necessary. An ovariohysterectomy is considered major surgery.

Neutering the male at a young age will inhibit some characteristic male behavior that owners frown upon. I have found my boys will not hike their legs and mark territory if they are neutered at six months of age. Also neutering at a young age has hormonal benefits, lessening the chance of hormonal aggressiveness.

Surgery involves removing the testicles but leaving the scrotum. If there should be a retained testicle, then he definitely needs to be neutered before the age of two or three years. Retained testicles can develop into cancer. Unneutered males are at risk for testicular cancer, perineal fistulas, perianal tumors and fistulas and prostatic disease.

Intact males and females are prone to housebreaking accidents. Females urinate frequently before, during and after heat cycles, and males tend to mark territory if there is a female in heat. Males may show the same behavior if there is a visiting dog or guests.

Surgery involves a sterile operating procedure equivalent to human surgery. The incision site is shaved, surgically scrubbed and draped. The veterinarian wears a sterile surgical gown, cap, mask and gloves. Anesthesia should be monitored by a registered technician. It is customary for the veterinarian to recommend a pre-anesthetic blood screening, looking for metabolic problems and a ECG rhythm strip to check for normal heart function. Today anesthetics are equal to human anesthetics, which enables your dog to walk out of the clinic the same day as surgery.

Some folks worry about their dog gaining weight after being neutered or spayed. This is usually not the case. It is true that some dogs may be less active so they could develop a problem, but my own dogs are just as active as they were before surgery. I have a hard time keeping weight on them. However, if your dog should begin to gain, then you need to decrease his food and see to it that he gets a little more exercise.

A healthy Aussie will have strong, powerful legs and should not favor one leg in his stride. Any irregularities in your dog's gait should be examined by your veterinarian.

Medical Problems

Anal Sacs

These are small sacs on either side of the rectum that can cause the dog discomfort when they are full. They should empty when the dog has a bowel movement. Symptoms of inflammation or impaction are excessive licking under the tail and/or a bloody or sticky discharge from the anal area. Breeders like myself recommend emptying the sacs on a regular schedule when bathing the dog. Many veterinarians prefer this isn't done unless there are symptoms. You can express the sacs by squeezing the two sacs (at the five and seven o'clock positions) in and up toward the anus. Take precautions not to get in the way of the foul-smelling fluid that is expressed. Some dogs object to this procedure so it would be wise to have someone hold the head. Scooting is caused by anal-sac irritation and not worms.

Colitis

The stool may be frank blood or blood tinged and is the result of inflammation of the colon. Colitis, sometimes intermittent, can be the result of stress, undiagnosed whipworms, or perhaps idiopathic (no explainable reason). I have had several dogs prone to this disorder. They felt fine and were willing to eat but would have intermittent bloody stools. If this in an ongoing problem, you should probably feed a diet higher in fiber. Seek professional help if your dog feels poorly and/or the condition persists.

Conjunctivitis

Many breeds are prone to this problem. The conjunctiva is the pink tissue that lines the inner surface of the eyeball except the clear, transparent cornea. Irritating substances such as bacteria, foreign matter or chemicals can cause it to become reddened and swollen. It is important to keep any hair trimmed from around the eyes. Long hair stays damp and aggravates the problem. Keep the eyes cleaned with warm water and wipe away any matter that has accumulated in the corner of the eyes. If the condition persists, you should see your veterinarian. This problem goes hand in hand with keratoconjunctivitis sicca.

Ear Infection

Otitis externa is an inflammation of the external ear canal that begins at the outside opening of the ear and extends inward to the eardrum. Dogs with pendulous ears are prone to this disease, but isn't it interesting that breeds with upright ears also have a high incidence of problems? Allergies, food and inhalent, along with hormonal problems, such as hypothyroidism, are major contributors to the disease. For those dogs which have recurring problems you need to investigate the underlying cause if you hope to cure them.

I recommend that you are careful never to get water into the ears. Water provides a great medium for bacteria to grow. If your dog swims or you inadvertently get water into his ears, then use a drying agent. An at-home preparation would be to use equal parts of three-percent hydrogen peroxide and 70-percent rubbing alcohol. Another preparation is equal parts of white vinegar and water. Your veterinarian alternatively can provide a suitable product. When cleaning the ears, be careful of using cotton tip applicators since they make it easy to pack debris down into the canal. Only clean what you can see.

If your dog has an ongoing infection, don't be surprised if your veterinarian recommends sedating him and flushing his ears with a bulb syringe. Sometimes this needs to be done a few times to get the ear clean. The ear must be clean so that medication can come in contact with the canal. Be prepared to return for rechecks until the infection is gone. This may involve more flushings if the ears are very bad.

For chronic or recurring cases, your veterinarian may recommend thyroid testing, etc., and a hypoallergenic diet for a trial period of 10 to 12 weeks. Depending on your dog, it may be a good idea to see a dermatologist. Ears shouldn't be taken lightly. If the condition gets out of hand, then surgery may be necessary. Please ask your veterinarian to explain proper ear maintenance for your dog.

Your Aussie pup should have clear eyes and a full, healthy coat.

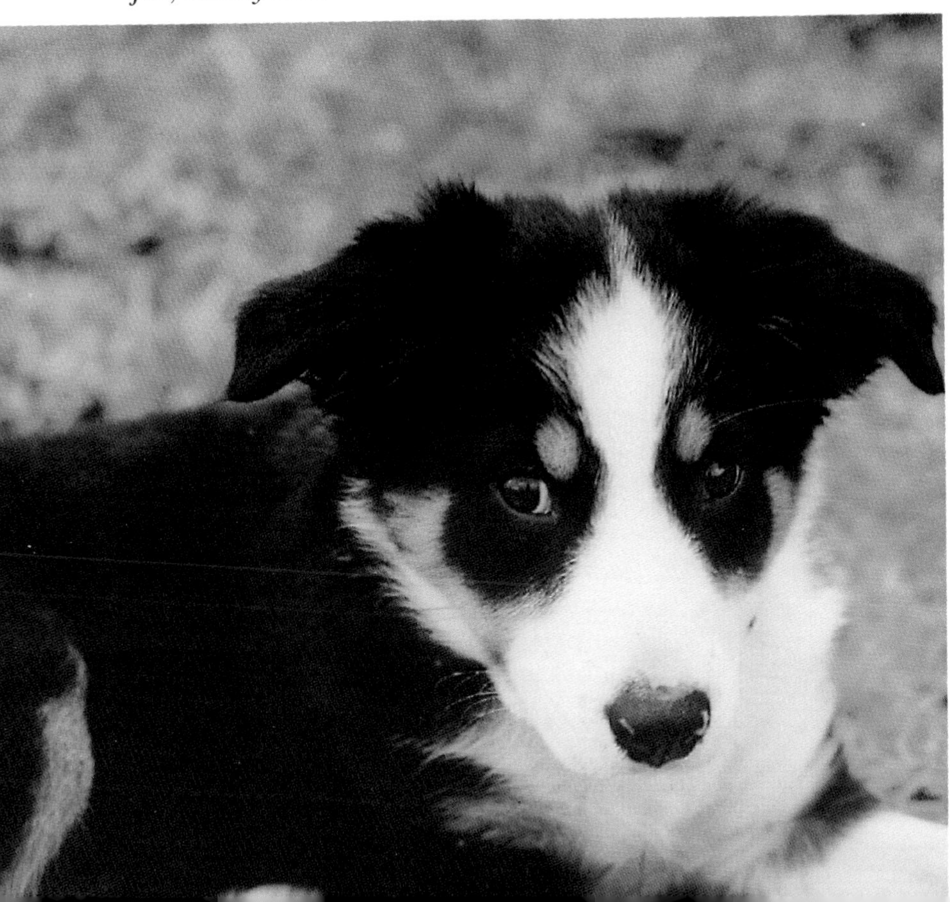

Flea Bite Allergy

This is the result of a hypersensitivity to the bite of a flea and its saliva. It only takes one bite to cause the dog to chew or scratch himself raw. Your dog may need medical attention to ease his discomfort. You need to clip the hair around the "hot spot" and wash it with a mild soap and water and you may need to do this daily if the area weeps. Apply an antibiotic anti-inflammatory product. Hot spots can occur from other trauma, such as grooming.

Interdigital Cysts

Check for these on your dog's feet if he shows signs of lameness. They are frequently associated with staph infections and can be quite painful. A home remedy is to soak the infected foot in a solution of a half teaspoon of bleach in a couple of quarts of water. Do this two to three times a day for a couple of days. Check with your veterinarian for an alternative remedy; antibiotics usually work well. If there is a recurring problem, surgery may be required.

Your Australian Shepherd will be happier and his teeth and gums healthier if you give him a souper-sized POPpup™ to chew on. Every POPpup™ is 100% edible and enhanced with dog-friendly ingredients like liver, cheese, spinach, chicken, carrots, or potatoes. In fact, their main ingredient is potato starch, which gives them a 3% protein content. What you won't find in a POPpup™ is salt, sugar, alcohol, plastic, or preservatives. You can even microwave a POPpup™ to turn it into a huge crackly treat for your Aussie to enjoy. Available at your local pet shop.

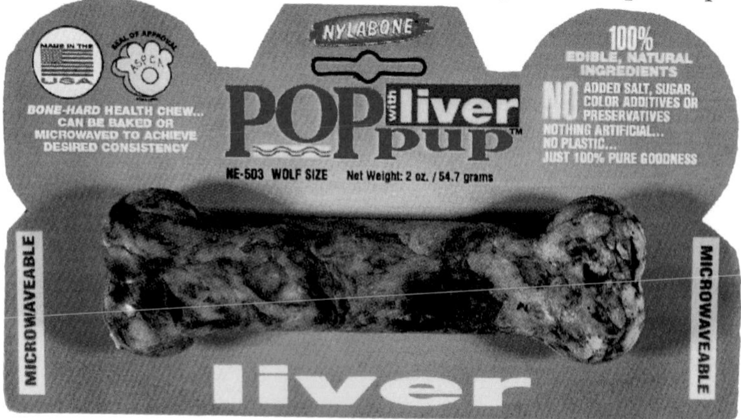

Lameness

It may only be an interdigital cyst or it could be a mat between the toes, especially if your dog licks his feet. Sometimes it is hard to determine which leg is affected. If he is holding up his leg, then you need to see your veterinarian.

The health of your Australian Shepherd will show in his overall appearance and attitude.

Skin

Frequently poor skin is the result of an allergy to fleas, an inhalant allergy or food allergy. These types of problems usually result in a staph dermatitis. Dogs with food allergy usually show signs of severe itching and scratching. However, I have had some dogs with food allergies that never once itched. Their only symptom was swelling of the ears with no ear infection. Food allergy may result in recurrent bacterial skin and ear infections. Your veterinarian or dermatologist will recommend a good restricted diet. It is not wise for you to hit and miss with different dog foods. Many of the diets offered over the counter are not the hypoallergenic diet you are led to believe. Dogs acquire allergies through exposure.

Inhalant allergies result in atopy, which causes licking of the feet, scratching the body and rubbing the muzzle. It may be seasonable. Your veterinarian or dermatologist can perform intradermal testing for inhalant allergies. If your dog should test positive, then a vaccine may be prepared. The results are very satisfying.

Tonsillitis

Usually young dogs have a higher incidence of this problem than the older ones. The older dogs have built up resistance. It is very contagious. Sometimes it is difficult to determine if it is tonsillitis or kennel cough since the symptoms are similar. Symptoms include fever, poor eating, swallowing with difficulty and retching up a white, frothy mucus.

DENTAL CARE for Your Dog's Life

So you've got a new puppy! You also have a new set of puppy teeth in your household. Anyone who has ever raised a puppy is abundantly aware of these new teeth. Your puppy will chew anything it can reach, chase your shoelaces, and play "tear the rag" with any piece of clothing it can find. When puppies are newly born, they have no teeth. At about four weeks of age, puppies of most breeds begin to develop their deciduous or baby teeth. They begin eating semi-solid food, fighting and biting with their litter mates, and learning discipline from their mother. As their new teeth come in, they inflict more pain on their mother's breasts, so her feeding sessions become less frequent and shorter. By six or eight weeks, the mother will start growling to warn her pups when they are fighting too roughly or hurting her as they nurse too much with their new teeth.

Let your dog do his part in his dental health by giving him a Plaque Attacker® from Nylabone®. The raised tips massage the gums and help keep the teeth clean as the dog chews.

Puppies need to chew. It is a necessary part of their physical and mental development. They develop muscles and necessary life skills as they drag objects around, fight over possession, and vocalize alerts and warnings. Puppies chew on things to explore their world. They are using their sense of taste to determine what is food and what is not. How else can they tell an electrical cord from a lizard? At about four months of age, most

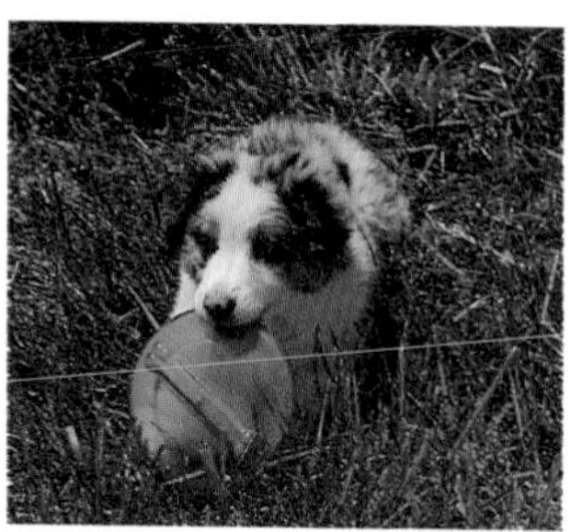

Your Aussie will be happy to fetch and retrieve a Gumabone® Frisbee®. Its got a texture he'll love to sink his teeth into, it's built to last, and the molded bone on top makes it easy for the dog to pick up.*

**The trademark Frisbee is used under license from Mattel, Inc. California, USA.*

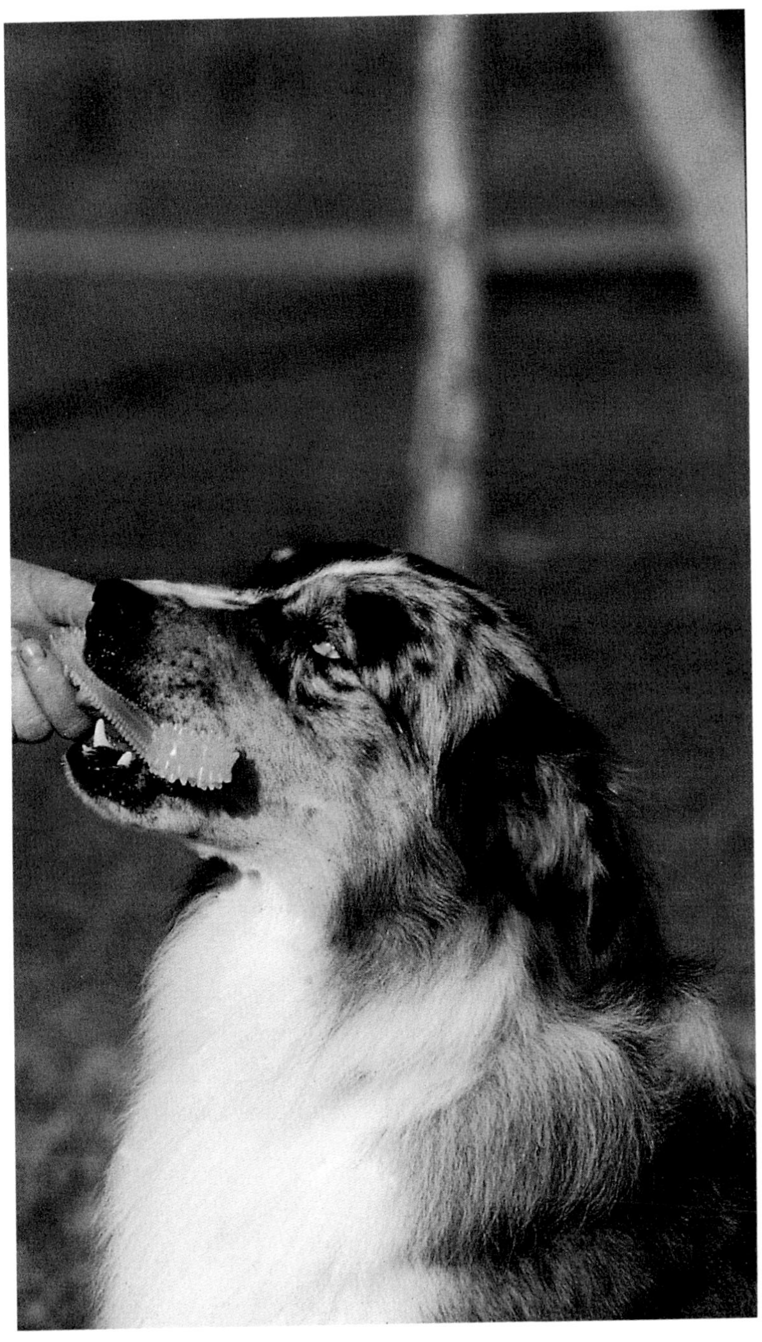

puppies begin shedding their baby teeth. Often these teeth need some help to come out and make way for the permanent teeth. The incisors (front teeth) will be replaced first. Then, the adult canine or fang teeth erupt. When the baby tooth is not shed before the permanent tooth comes in, veterinarians call it a retained deciduous tooth. This condition will often cause gum infections by trapping hair and debris between the permanent tooth and the retained baby tooth. Nylafloss® is an excellent device for puppies to use. They can toss it, drag it, and chew on the many surfaces it presents. The baby teeth can catch in the nylon material, aiding in their removal. Puppies that have adequate chew toys will have less destructive behavior, develop more physically, and have less chance of retained deciduous teeth.

During the first year, your dog should be seen by your veterinarian at regular intervals. Your veterinarian will let you know when to bring in your puppy for vaccinations and parasite examinations. At each visit, your veterinarian should inspect the lips, teeth, and mouth as part of a complete physical examination. You

Your veterinarian should check your Australian Shepherd's teeth, mouth and lips as part of his complete annual examination.

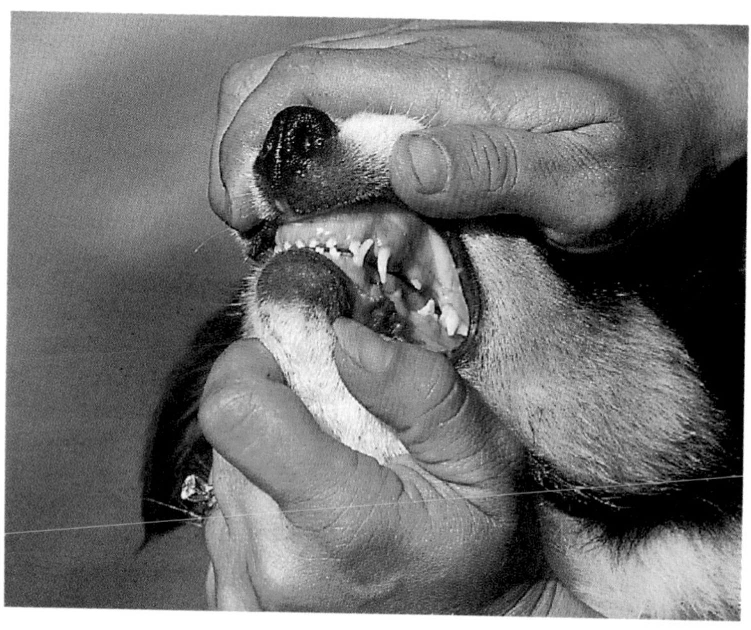

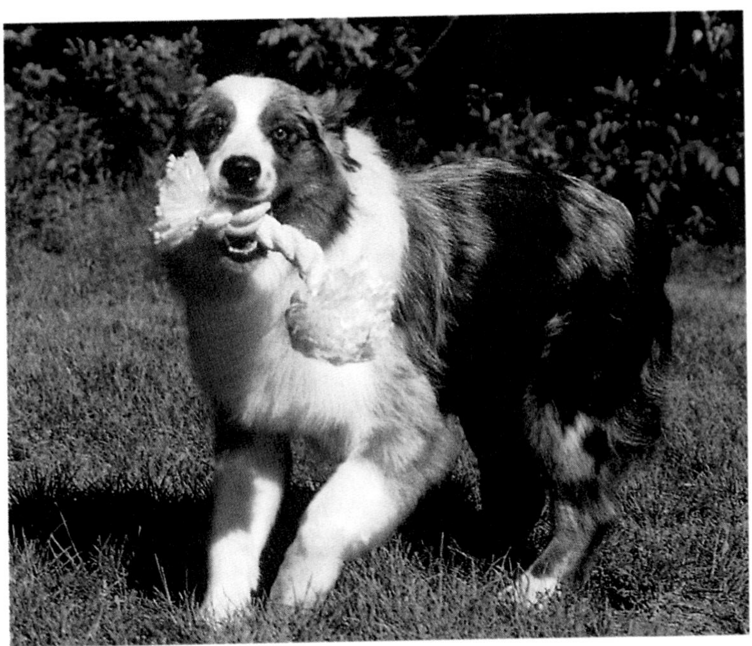

Your Aussie will enjoy hours of fun with Nylafloss®, a great tug toy that will literally floss his teeth while he plays.

should take some part in the maintenance of your dog's oral health. You should examine your dog's mouth weekly throughout his first year to make sure there are no sores, foreign objects, tooth problems, etc. If your dog drools excessively, shakes its head, or has bad breath, consult your veterinarian. By the time your dog is six months old, the permanent teeth are all in and plaque can start to accumulate on the tooth surfaces. This is when your dog needs to develop good dental-care habits to prevent calculus build-up on its teeth. Brushing is best. That is a fact that cannot be denied. However, some dogs do not like their teeth brushed regularly, or you may not be able to accomplish the task. In that case, you should consider a product that will help prevent plaque and calculus build-up.

The Plaque Attackers® and Galileo Bone® are other excellent choices for the first three years of a dog's life. Their shapes make them interesting for the dog. As the dog chews on them, the solid polyurethane massages the gums which improves the blood circulation to the periodontal tissues. Projections on the chew devices increase the surface and are in contact with the tooth for more efficient cleaning. The unique shape and consistency prevent your dog from exerting excessive force on his own teeth or from breaking off pieces of the bone. If your dog is an aggressive chewer or weighs more than 55 pounds (25 kg), you should consider giving him a Nylabone®, the most durable chew product on the market.

The Gumabone®, made by the Nylabone Company, is constructed of strong polyurethane, which is softer than nylon. Less powerful chewers prefer the Gumabones® to the Nylabones®. A super option for your dog is the Hercules Bone®, a uniquely shaped bone named after the great Olympian for its exception strength. Like all Nylabone products, they are specially scented to make them attractive to your dog. Ask your veterinarian about these bones and he will validate the good doctor's prescription: Nylabones® not only give your dog a good chewing workout but also help to save your dog's teeth (and even his life, as it protects him from possible fatal periodontal diseases).

By the time dogs are four years old, 75% of them have periodontal disease. It is the most common infection in dogs. Yearly examinations by your veterinarian are essential to maintaining your dog's good health. If your veterinarian detects periodontal disease, he or she may recommend a prophylactic cleaning. To do a thorough cleaning, it will be necessary to put your dog under anesthesia. With modern gas anesthetics and monitoring equipment, the procedure is pretty safe. Your veterinarian will scale the teeth with an ultrasound scaler or hand instrument. This removes the calculus from the teeth. If there are calculus deposits below the gum line, the veterinarian will plane the roots to make them smooth. After

Aggressive chewers like the Australian Shepherd will benefit from the Nylabone® Wishbone®, a fun-shaped durable chew product.

all of the calculus has been removed, the teeth are polished with pumice in a polishing cup. If any medical or surgical treatment is needed, it is done at this time. The final step would be fluoride treatment and your follow-up treatment at home. If the periodontal disease is advanced, the veterinarian may prescribe a medicated mouth rinse or antibiotics for use at home. Make sure your dog has safe, clean and attractive chew toys and treats. Chooz® treats are another way of using a consumable treat to help keep your dog's teeth clean.

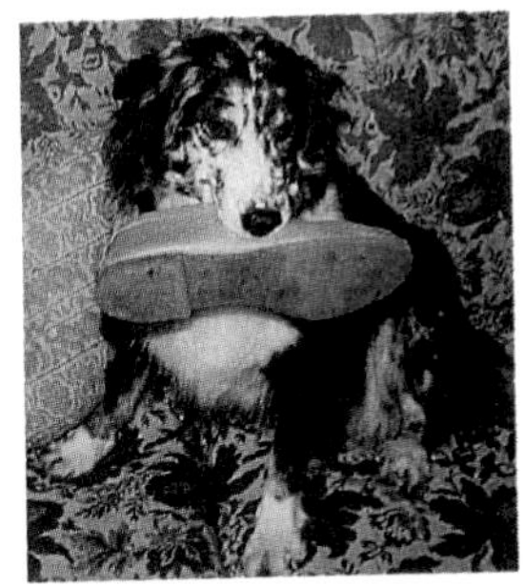

Give your Australian Shepherd puppy plenty of Nylabones® to play with or he might resort to chewing on things he's not supposed to - like your shoes!

Why will you want to give your Australian Shepherd a medium-sized Carrot Bone™? Because you know carrots are rich in fiber, carbohydrates and vitamin A. Because it's a durable chew containing no plastics or artificial ingredients of any kind. Because it can be served as-is, in a bone-hard form, or microwaved to a biscuity consistency - whichever your Aussie prefers. Because it's a 100% natural plaque, obesity and boredom fighter for your Aussie. Available at your local pet shop.

Rawhide is the most popular of all materials for a dog to chew. This has never been good

news to dog owners, because rawhide is inherently very dangerous for dogs. Thousands of dogs have died from rawhide, having swallowed the hide after it has become soft and mushy, only to cause stomach and intestinal blockage. A new rawhide product on the market has finally solved the problem of rawhide: molded Roar-Hide® from Nylabone. These are composed of processed, cut up, and melted American rawhide injected into your dog's favorite shape: a dog bone. These dog-safe devices smell and taste like rawhide but don't break up. The ridges on the bones help to fight tartar build-up on the teeth and they last ten times longer than the usual rawhide chews.

As your dog ages, professional examination and cleaning should become more frequent. The mouth should be inspected at least once a year. Your veterinarian may recommend visits every six months. In the geriatric patient, organs such as the heart, liver, and kidneys do not function as well as when they were young. Your veterinarian will probably

To combat boredom and relieve your Aussie's natural desire to chew, there's nothing better than a Roarhide®. Unlike common rawhide, this bone won't turn into a gooey mess when chewed on, so your dog won't choke on small pieces of it, and your carpet won't be stained by it. The Roarhide® is completely edible and is high protein (over 86%) and low in fat (less than one-third of one percent). The regular-sized Roarhide® is just right for your Aussie. Available at your local pet shop.

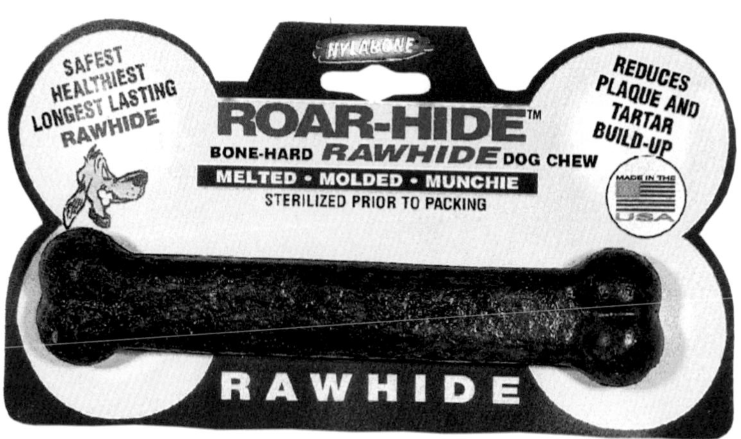

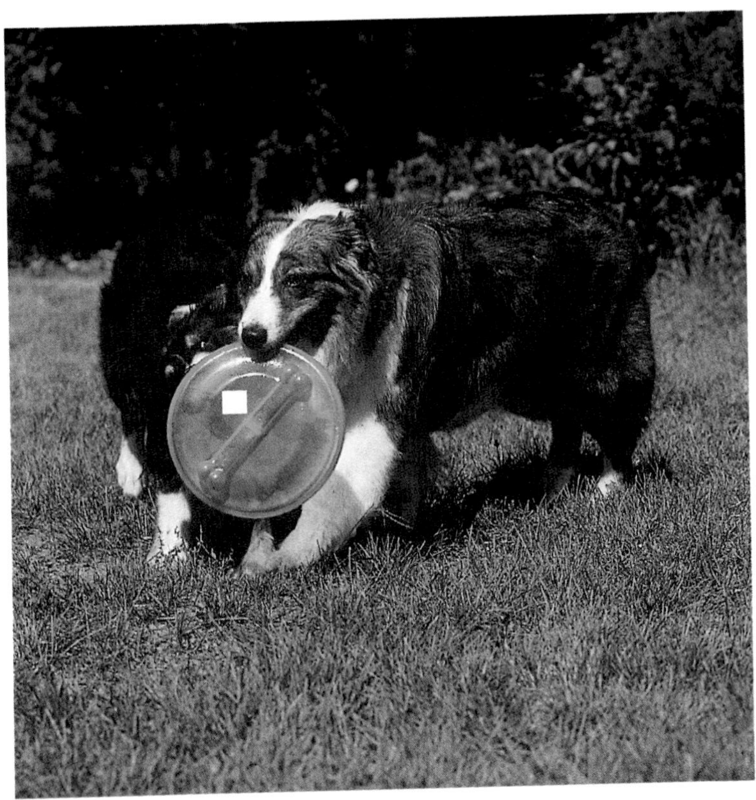

With a variety of Gumabones® to play with, these Aussies are sure to have strong teeth and gums.

want to test these organs' functions prior to using general anesthesia for dental cleaning. If your dog is a good chewer and you work closely with your veterinarian, your dog can keep all of its teeth all of its life. However, as your dog ages, his sense of smell, sight, and taste will diminish. He may not have the desire to chase, trap or chew his toys. He will also not have the energy to chew for long periods, as arthritis and periodontal disease make chewing painful. This will leave you with more responsibility for keeping his teeth clean and healthy. The dog that would not let you brush his teeth at one year of age, may let you brush his teeth now that he is ten years old.

If you train your dog with good chewing habits as a puppy, he will have healthier teeth throughout his life.

IDENTIFICATION and Finding the Lost Dog

There are several ways of identifying your dog. The old standby is a collar with dog license, rabies, and ID tags. Unfortunately collars have a way of being separated from the dog and tags fall off. I am not suggesting you shouldn't use a collar and tags. If they stay intact and on the dog, they are the quickest way of identification.

For several years owners have been tattooing their dogs. Some tattoos use a number with a registry. Here lies the problem because there are several registries to check. If you wish to tattoo, use your social security number. The humane shelters have the means to trace it. It is usually done on the inside of the rear thigh. The area is first shaved and numbed. There is no pain, although a few dogs do not like the buzzing sound. Occasionally tattooing is not legible and needs to be redone.

The newest method of identification is microchipping. The microchip is a computer chip that is no larger than a grain of rice. The veterinarian implants it by injection between the shoulder blades. The dog feels no discomfort. If your dog is lost and picked up by the humane society, they can trace you by scanning the microchip, which has its own code. Microchip scanners are friendly to other brands of microchips and their registries. The microchip comes with a dog tag saying the dog

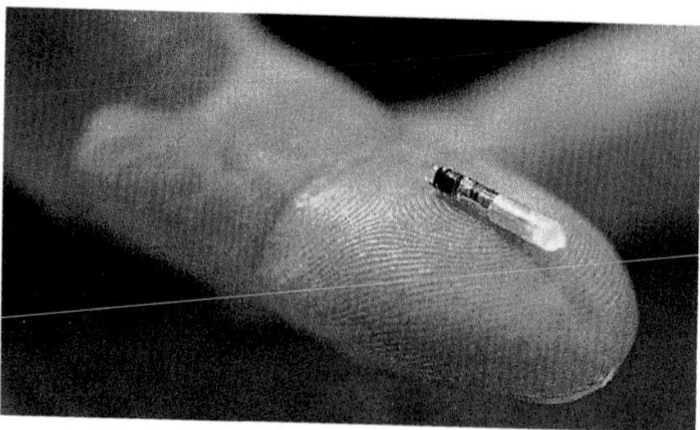

The newest method of identification is microchipping. The microchip is a computer chip that is no bigger than a grain of rice.

is microchipped. It is the safest way of identifying your dog.

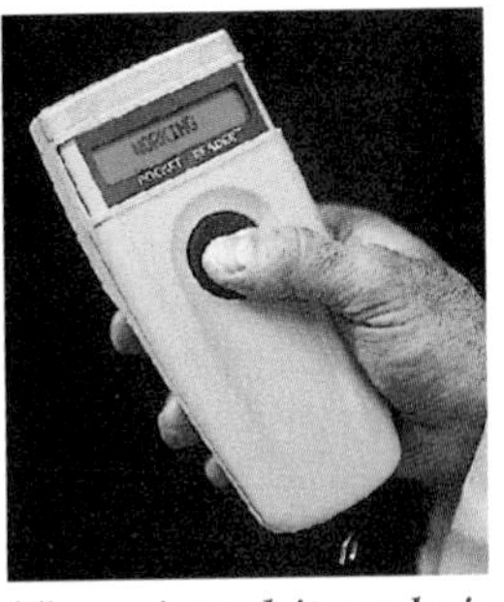

The microchip code is picked up by a scanner, and the code traces the lost dog back to his owner.

Finding The Lost Dog

I am sure you will agree with me that there would be little worse than losing your dog. Responsible pet owners rarely lose their dogs. They do not let their dogs run free because they don't want harm to come to them. Not only that but in most, if not all, states there is a leash law.

Beware of fenced-in yards. They can be a hazard. Dogs find ways to escape

If you leave your Australians Shepherds outside unsupervised, make sure they are enclosed in a secure area so they will not become lost or stolen.

either over or under the fence. Another fast exit is through the gate that perhaps the neighbor's child left unlocked.

Below is a list that hopefully will be of help to you if you need it. Remember don't give up, keep looking. Your dog is worth your efforts.

1. Contact your neighbors and put flyers with a photo on it in their mailboxes. Information you should include would be the dog's name, breed, sex, color, age, source of identification, when your dog was last seen and where, and your name and phone numbers. It may be helpful to say the dog needs medical care. Offer a *reward*.

Make sure you have a good, clear photograph of your Australian Shepherd to distribute in case you become separated from your pet.

2. Check all local shelters daily. It is also possible for your dog to be picked up away from home and end up in an out-of-the-way shelter. Check these too. Go in person. It is not good enough to call. Most shelters are limited on the time they can hold dogs then they are put up for adoption or euthanized. There is the possibility that your dog will not make it to the shelter for several days. Your dog could have been wandering or someone may have tried to keep him.
3. Notify all local veterinarians. Call and send flyers.
4. Call your breeder. Frequently breeders are contacted when one of their breed is found.
5. Contact the rescue group for your breed.
6. Contact local schools–children may have seen your dog.
7. Post flyers at the schools, groceries, gas stations, convenience stores, veterinary clinics, groomers and any other place that will allow them.

8. Advertise in the newspaper.
9. Advertise on the radio.

Most people, like the Densins of Canada, consider their Aussies to be valued family members and will conduct extensive searches for their lost pets.

TRAVELING with Your Dog

The earlier you start traveling with your new puppy or dog, the better. He needs to become accustomed to traveling. However, some dogs are nervous riders and become carsick easily. It is helpful if he starts with an empty stomach. Do not despair, as it will go better if you continue taking him with you on short fun rides. How would you feel if every time you rode in the car you stopped at the doctor's for an injection? You would soon dread that nasty car. Older dogs that tend to get carsick may have more of a problem adjusting to traveling. Those dogs that are having a serious problem may benefit from some medication prescribed by the veterinarian.

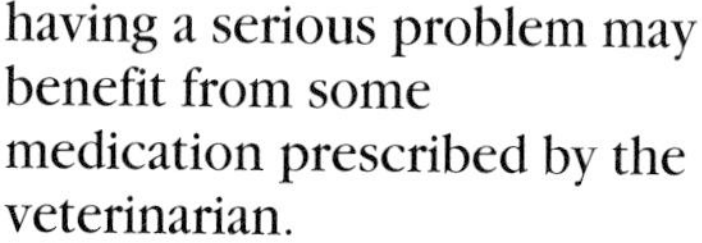

You don't have to leave your Australian Shepherd at home when you travel if you find accommodations that will accept your dog.

Do give your dog a chance to relieve himself before getting into the car. It is a good idea to be prepared for a clean up with a leash, paper towels, bag and terry cloth towel.

The safest place for your dog is in a fiberglass crate, although close confinement can promote carsickness in some dogs. If your dog is nervous you can try letting him ride on the seat next to you or in someone's lap.

An alternative to the crate would be to use a car harness made for dogs and/or a safety strap attached to the harness or collar. Whatever you do, do not let your dog ride in the back of a pickup truck unless he is securely tied on a very short lead. I've seen trucks stop quickly and, even though the dog was tied, it fell out and was dragged.

Never allow your Australian Shepherd to ride in the back of a pick-up truck unless he is in a crate. He might jump out and injure himself.

I do occasionally let my dogs ride loose with me because I really enjoy their companionship, but in all honesty they are safer in their crates. I have a friend whose van rolled in an accident but his dogs, in their fiberglass crates, were not injured nor did they escape. Another advantage of the crate is that it is a safe place to leave him if you need to run into the store. Otherwise you wouldn't be able to leave the windows down. Keep in mind that while many dogs are overly protective in their crates, this may not be enough to deter dognappers. In some states it is against the law to leave a dog in the car unattended.

Never leave a dog loose in the car wearing a collar and leash. I have known more than one dog that has killed himself by hanging. Do not let him put his head out an open window. Foreign debris can be blown into his eyes. When leaving your dog unattended in a car, consider the temperature. It can take

less than five minutes to reach temperatures over 100 degrees Fahrenheit.

Trips

Perhaps you are taking a trip. Give consideration to what is best for your dog–traveling with you or boarding. When traveling by car, van or motor home, you need to think ahead about locking your vehicle. In all probability you have many valuables in the car and do not wish to leave it unlocked. Perhaps most valuable and not replaceable is your dog. Give thought to securing your vehicle and providing adequate ventilation for him. Another consideration for you when traveling with your dog is medical problems that may arise and little inconveniences, such as exposure to external parasites. Some areas of the country are quite flea infested. You may want to carry flea spray with you. This is even a good idea when staying in motels. Quite possibly you are not the only occupant of the room.

Dogs who travel often, like this one at an obedience trial, come to enjoy the ever-changing life on the road.

Unbelievably many motels and even hotels do allow canine guests, even some very first-class ones. Gaines Pet Foods Corporation publishes *Touring With Towser*, a directory of domestic hotels and motels that accommodate guests with dogs. Their address is Gaines TWT, PO Box 5700, Kankakee, IL, 60902. I would recommend you call ahead to any motel that you may be considering and see if they accept pets. Sometimes it is necessary to pay a deposit against room damage. Of course you are more likely to gain accommodations for a small dog than a large dog. Also the management feels reassured when you mention that your dog will be crated. Since my dogs tend to bark when I leave the room, I leave the TV on nearly full blast to deaden the noises outside that tend to encourage my dogs to bark. If you do travel with your dog, take along plenty of baggies so that you can clean up after him. When we all do our

This is Mesa at nine weeks, ready for her first ride in the car - wearing a safety harness, of course! Owners, Steve and Carol Maslansky.

When you travel with your Australian Shepherd, bring familiar things with you, like his crate and toys, to make him feel at home.

share in cleaning up, we make it possible for motels to continue accepting our pets. As a matter of fact, you should practice cleaning up everywhere you take your dog.

Depending on where your are traveling, you may need an up-to-date health certificate issued by your veterinarian. It is good policy to take along your dog's medical information, which would include the name, address and phone number of your veterinarian, vaccination record, rabies certificate, and any medication he is taking.

AIR TRAVEL

When traveling by air, you need to contact the airlines to check their policy. Usually you have to make arrangements up to a couple of weeks in advance for traveling with your dog. The airlines require your dog to travel in an airline approved fiberglass crate. Usually these can be purchased through the airlines but they are also readily available in most pet-supply stores. If your dog is not accustomed to a crate, then it is a good idea to get him acclimated to it before your trip. The day of the actual trip you should withhold water about one hour ahead of departure and no food for about 12 hours. The airlines generally have temperature restrictions, which do not allow pets to travel if it is either too cold or too hot. Frequently these restrictions are based on the temperatures at the departure and arrival airports. It's best to inquire about a health certificate. These usually need to be issued within ten days of departure. You should arrange for non-stop, direct flights and if a commuter plane should be involved, check to see if it will carry dogs. Some don't. The Humane Society of the United States has put together a tip sheet for airline traveling. You can receive a copy by sending a self-addressed stamped envelope to:

The Humane Society of the United States
Tip Sheet
2100 L Street NW
Washington, DC 20037.

The more accustomed your Aussie is to traveling, the more willing he will be to follow you anywhere.

Regulations differ for traveling outside of the country and are sometimes changed without notice. Well in advance you need to write or call the appropriate consulate or agricultural department for instructions. Some countries have lengthy quarantines (six months), and countries differ in their rabies vaccination requirements. For instance, it may have to be given at least 30 days ahead of your departure.

Do make sure your dog is wearing proper identification. You never know when you might be in an accident and separated from your dog. Or your dog could be frightened and somehow manage to escape and run away. When I travel, my dogs wear collars with engraved nameplates with my name, phone number and city.

Another suggestion would be to carry in-case-of-emergency instructions. These would include the address and phone number of a relative or friend, your veterinarian's name, address and phone number, and your dog's medical information.

BOARDING KENNELS

Because they are such accommodating dogs, Australian Shepherds usually fare well on vacations.

Perhaps you have decided that you need to board your dog. Your veterinarian can recommend a good boarding facility or possibly a pet sitter that will come to your house. It is customary for the boarding kennel to ask for proof of vaccination for the DHLPP, rabies and bordetella vaccine. The bordetella should have been given within six months of boarding. This is for your protection. If they do not ask for this proof I would not board at their kennel. Ask about flea control. Those dogs that suffer flea-bite allergy can get in trouble at a boarding kennel. Unfortunately boarding kennels are limited on how much they are able to do.

For more information on pet sitting, contact NAPPS:
National Association of Professional Pet Sitters
1200 G Street, NW
Suite 760
Washington, DC 20005.

Our clinic has technicians that pet sit and technicians that board clinic patients in their homes. This may be an alternative for you. Ask your veterinarian if they have an employee that can help you. There is a definite advantage of having a technician care for your dog, especially if your dog is on medication or is a senior citizen.

You can write for a copy of *Traveling With Your Pet* from ASPCA, Education Department, 441 E. 92nd Street, New York, NY 10128.

A reputable boarding kennel will require that dogs receive the vaccination for kennel cough no less than two weeks before their scheduled stay.

BEHAVIOR and Canine Communication

Studies of the human/animal bond point out the importance of the unique relationships that exist between people and their pets. Those of us who share our lives with pets understand the special part they play through companionship, service and protection.

Senior citizens show more concern for their own eating habits when they have the responsibility of feeding a dog. Seeing that their dog is routinely exercised encourages the owner to think of schedules that otherwise may seem unimportant to the senior citizen. The older owner may be arthritic and feeling poorly but with responsibility for his dog he has a reason to get up and get moving. It is a big plus if his dog is an attention seeker who will demand such from his owner.

Over the last couple of decades, it has been shown that pets relieve the stress of those who lead busy lives. Owning a pet has been known to lessen the occurrence of heart attack and stroke.

Many single folks thrive on the companionship of a dog. Lifestyles are very different from a long time ago, and today more individuals seek the single life. However, they receive fulfillment from owning a dog.

Most likely the majority of our dogs live in family environments. The companionship they provide is well worth the effort involved. In my opinion, every child should have the opportunity to have a family dog. Dogs teach responsibility through understanding their care, feelings

It has been found that spending time with a dog can reduce stress and improve your quality of life. Who can resist smiling at this adorable Aussie?

Australian Shepherds enrich the lives of their owners by being loving and faithful companions. This is Jason, Jeremy and Jessica McDaniel with their friend Levi.

and even respecting their life cycles. Frequently those children who have not been exposed to dogs grow up afraid of dogs, which isn't good. Dogs sense timidity and some will take advantage of the situation.

Today more dogs are serving as service dogs. Since the origination of the Seeing Eye dogs years ago, we now have trained hearing dogs. Also dogs are trained to provide service for the handicapped and are able to perform many different tasks for their owners. Search and Rescue dogs, with their handlers, are sent throughout the world to assist in recovery of disaster victims. They are life savers.

Therapy dogs are very popular with nursing homes, and some hospitals even allow them to visit. The inhabitants truly look forward to their visits. I have taken a couple of my dogs visiting and left in tears when I saw the response of the patients. They wanted and were allowed to have my dogs in their beds to hold and love.

Many people thrive on the devoted companionship that an Australian Shepherd can provide.

Nationally there is a Pet Awareness Week to educate students and others about the value and basic care of our pets. Many countries take an even greater interest in their pets than Americans do. In those countries the pets are allowed to accompany their owners into restaurants and shops, etc. In the U.S. this freedom is only available to our service dogs. Even so we think very highly of the human/animal bond.

CANINE BEHAVIOR

Canine behavior problems are the number-one reason for pet owners to dispose of their dogs, either through new homes, humane shelters or euthanasia. Unfortunately there are too many owners who are unwilling to devote the necessary time to properly train their dogs. On the other hand, there are those who not only are concerned about inherited health problems but are also aware of the dog's mental stability.

You may realize that a breed and his group relatives (i.e.,

sporting, hounds, etc.) show tendencies to behavioral characteristics. An experienced breeder can acquaint you with his breed's personality. Unfortunately many breeds are labeled with poor temperaments when actually the breed as a whole is not affected but only a small percentage of individuals within the breed.

If the breed in question is very popular, then of course there may be a higher number of unstable dogs. Do not label a breed good or bad. I know of absolutely awful-tempered dogs within one of our most popular, lovable breeds.

Inheritance and environment contribute to the dog's behavior. Some naïve people suggest inbreeding as the cause of bad temperaments. Inbreeding only results in poor behavior if the ancestors carry the trait. If there are excellent temperaments behind the dogs, then inbreeding will promote good temperaments in the offspring. Did you ever consider that inbreeding is what sets the characteristics of a breed? A purebred dog is the end result of inbreeding. This does not spare the mixed-breed dog from the same problems. Mixed-breed dogs frequently are the offspring of purebred dogs.

Every Aussie is an individual with a personality all his own. Some, like this Aussie puppy, might even start thinking they're human!

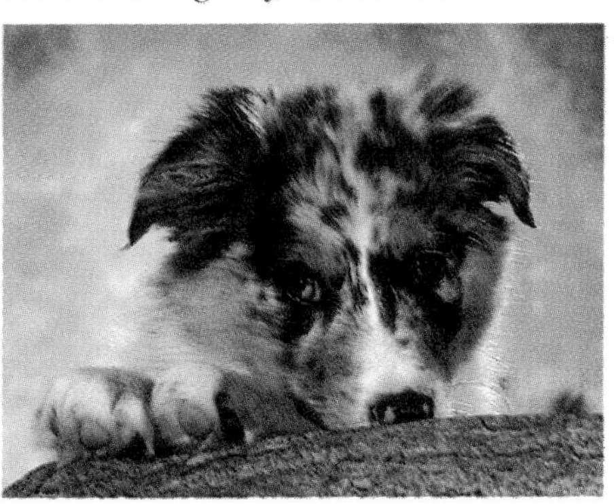

When planning a breeding, I like to observe the potential stud and his offspring in the show ring. If I see unruly behavior, I try to look into it further. I want to know if it is genetic or environmental, due to the lack of training and socialization. A good breeder will avoid breeding mentally unsound dogs.

Not too many decades ago most of our dogs led a different lifestyle than what is prevalent today. Usually mom stayed home so the dog had human companionship and someone to discipline it if needed. Not much was expected from the dog. Today's mom works and everyone's life is at a much faster pace.

The dog may have to adjust to being a "weekend" dog. The family is gone all day during the week, and the dog is left to his own devices for entertainment. Some dogs sleep all day waiting for their family to come home and others become wigwam wreckers if given the opportunity. Crates do ensure the safety of the dog and the house. However, he could become a physically and emotionally cripple if he doesn't get enough exercise and attention. We still appreciate and want the companionship of our dogs although we expect more from them. In many cases we tend to forget dogs are just that–*dogs* not human beings.

I own several dogs who are left crated during the day but I do try to make time for them in the evenings and on the weekends. Also we try to do something together before I leave for work. Maybe it helps them to have the companionship of other dogs. They accept their crates as their personal "houses" and seem to be content with their routine and thrive on trying their best to please me.

SOCIALIZING AND TRAINING

Many prospective puppy buyers lack experience regarding the proper socialization and training needed to develop the type of pet we all desire. In the first 18 months, training does take some work. Trust me, it is easier to start proper training before there is a problem that needs to be corrected.

The initial work begins with the breeder. The breeder should start socializing the puppy at five to six weeks of age and cannot let up. Human socializing is critical up through 12 weeks of age and likewise important during the following months. The litter should be left together during the first few weeks but it is necessary to separate them by ten weeks of age. Leaving them together after that time will increase competition for litter dominance. If puppies are not socialized with people by 12 weeks of age, they will be timid in later life.

The eight- to ten-week age period is a fearful time for puppies. They need to be handled very gently around children and adults. There should be no harsh discipline during this time. Starting at 14 weeks of age, the puppy begins the juvenile period, which ends when he reaches sexual maturity around six to 14 months of age. During the juvenile period he needs to be introduced to strangers (adults, children and other dogs) on the home property. At sexual maturity he will begin to bark at strangers and become more protective. Males start to lift their legs to urinate but if you desire you can inhibit this behavior by walking your boy on leash away from trees, shrubs, fences, etc.

Perhaps you are thinking about an older puppy. You need to inquire about the puppy's social experience. If he has lived in a kennel, he may have a hard time adjusting to people and environmental stimuli. Assuming he has had a good social upbringing, there are advantages to an older puppy.

Training includes puppy kindergarten and a minimum of one to two basic training classes. During these classes you will learn how to dominate your youngster. This is especially important if you own a

One of the most important aspects in a puppy's upbringing is socialization. Your Australian Shepherd should meet all kinds of animals while growing up.

large breed of dog. It is somewhat harder, if not nearly impossible, for some owners to be the Alpha figure when their dog towers over them. You will be taught how to properly restrain your dog. This concept is important. Again it puts you in the Alpha position. All dogs need to be restrained many times during their lives. Believe it or not, some of our worst offenders are the eight-week-old puppies that are brought to our clinic. They need to be gently restrained for a nail trim but the way they carry on you would think we were killing them. In comparison, their vaccination is a "piece of cake." When we ask dogs to do something that is not agreeable to them, then their worst comes out. Life will be easier for your dog if you expose him at a young age to the necessities of life–proper behavior and restraint.

UNDERSTANDING THE DOG'S LANGUAGE

Most authorities agree that the dog is a descendent of the wolf. The dog and wolf have similar traits. For instance both are pack oriented and prefer not to be isolated for long periods of time. Another characteristic is that the dog, like the wolf, looks to the leader–Alpha–for direction. Both the wolf and the dog

Even the most adorable puppies can develop behavior problems, which is why it is important to be a firm and fair owner.

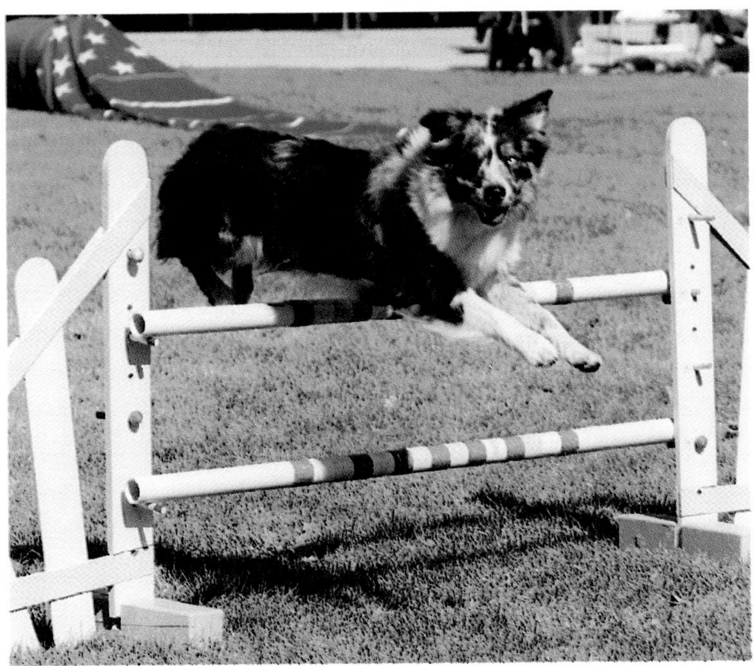

Aussies are high-energy, athletic dogs that can be taught to excel at many different activities when properly trained. This handsome dog conquers the agility high jump with ease.

communicate through body language, not only within their pack but with outsiders.

Every pack has an Alpha figure. The dog looks to you, or should look to you, to be that leader. If your dog doesn't receive the proper training and guidance, he very well may replace you as Alpha. This would be a serious problem and is certainly a disservice to your dog.

Eye contact is one way the Alpha wolf keeps order within his pack. You are Alpha so you must establish eye contact with your puppy. Obviously your puppy will have to look at you. Practice eye contact even if you need to hold his head for five to ten seconds at a time. You can give him a treat as a reward. Make sure your eye contact is gentle and not threatening. Later, if he has been naughty, it is permissible to give him a long, penetrating look. I caution you there are some older dogs that never learned eye contact as puppies and cannot accept eye contact. You should avoid eye contact with these dogs since they feel threatened and will retaliate as such.

BODY LANGUAGE

The Australian Shepherd must recognize his owner as the "leader of the pack" and dominant force or behavior problems may occur.

The play bow, when the forequarters are down and the hindquarters are elevated, is an invitation to play. Puppies play fight, which helps them learn the acceptable limits of biting. This is necessary for later in their lives. Nevertheless, an owner may be falsely reassured by the playful nature of his dog's aggression. Playful aggression toward another dog or human may be an indication of serious aggression in the future. Owners should never play fight or play tug-of-war with any dog that is inclined to be dominant.

Signs of submission are:

1. Avoids eye contact.
2. Active submission–the dog crouches down, ears back and the tail is lowered.
3. Passive submission–the dog rolls on his side with his hindlegs in the air and frequently urinates.

Signs of dominance are:

1. Makes eye contact.
2. Stands with ears up, tail up and the hair raised on his neck.
3. Shows dominance over another dog by standing at right angles over it.

Dominant dogs tend to behave in characteristic ways such as:

1. The dog may be unwilling to move from his place (i.e., reluctant to give up the sofa if the owner wants to sit there).
2. He may not part with toys or objects in his mouth and may show possessiveness with his food bowl.

This Aussie is using the play bow to invite his owner to have some fun. A dog's body language is a key to interpreting his feelings and actions.

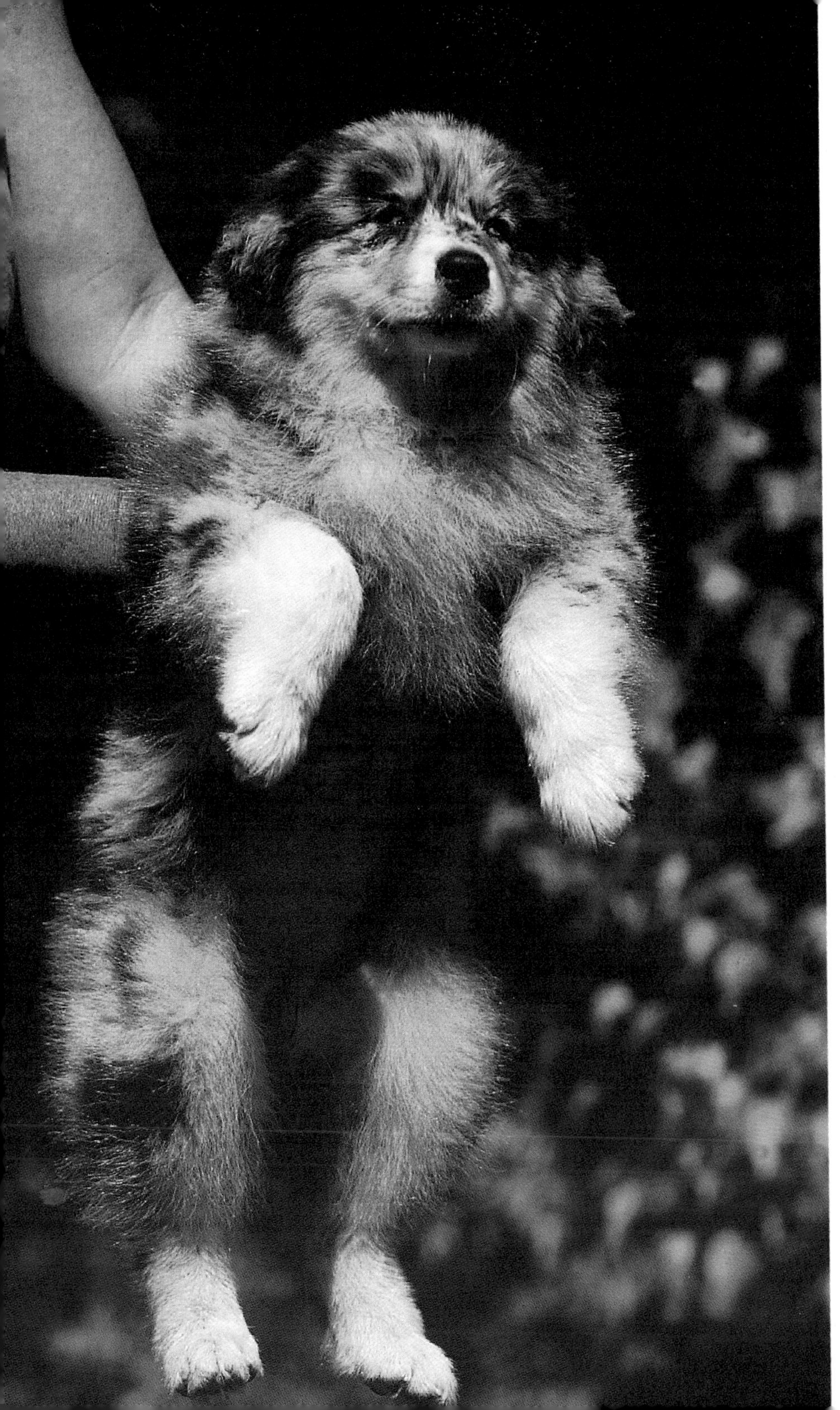

3. He may not respond quickly to commands.
4. He may be disagreeable for grooming and dislikes to be petted.

Dogs are popular because of their sociable nature. Those that have contact with humans during the first 12 weeks of life regard them as a member of their own species–their pack. All dogs have the potential for both dominant and submissive behavior. Only through experience and training do they learn to whom it is appropriate to show which behavior. Not all dogs are concerned with dominance but owners need to be aware of that potential. It is wise for the owner to establish his dominance early on.

The reluctance to part with toys or chews when commanded may signal that the dog is not submissive to his owner. Your Aussie should give up his toys when you tell him to.

A human can express dominance or submission toward a dog in the following ways:

1. Meeting the dog's gaze signals dominance. Averting the gaze signals submission. If the dog growls or threatens, averting the gaze is the first avoiding action to take–it may prevent attack. It is important to establish eye contact in the puppy. The older dog that has not been exposed to eye contact may see it as a threat and will not be willing to submit.
2. Being taller than the dog signals dominance; being lower signals submission. This is why, when attempting to make friends with a strange dog or catch the runaway, one should kneel down to his level. Some owners see their dogs become dominant when allowed on the furniture or on the bed. Then he is at the owner's level.
3. An owner can gain dominance by ignoring all the dog's social initiatives. The owner pays attention to the dog only when he obeys a command.

No dog should be allowed to achieve dominant status over any adult or child. Ways of preventing are as follows:

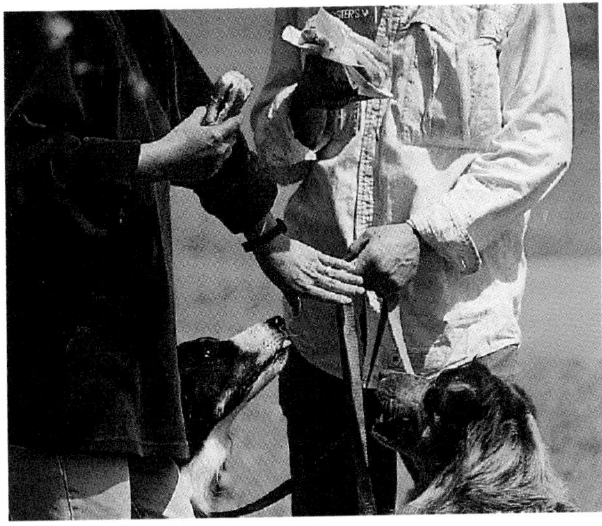

Dogs love to eat "people" food but must be taught not to grab or beg. Good manners are an important trait for your Australian Shepherd to possess.

1. Handle the puppy gently, especially during the three- to four-month period.
2. Let the children and adults handfeed him and teach him to take food without lunging or grabbing.
3. Do not allow him to chase children or joggers.
4. Do not allow him to jump on people or mount their legs. Even females may be inclined to mount. It is not only a male habit.
5. Do not allow him to growl for any reason.
6. Don't participate in wrestling or tug-of-war games.
7. Don't physically punish puppies for aggressive behavior. Restrain him from repeating the infraction and teach an alternative behavior. Dogs should earn everything they receive from their owners. This would include sitting to receive petting or treats, sitting before going out the door and sitting to receive the collar and leash. These types of exercises reinforce the owner's dominance.

Young children should never be left alone with a dog. It is important that children learn some basic obedience commands so they have some control over the dog. They will gain the respect of their dog.

Fear

One of the most common problems dogs experience is

being fearful. Some dogs are more afraid than others. On the lesser side, which is sometimes humorous to watch, my dog can be afraid of a strange object. He acts silly when something is out of place in the house. I call his problem perceptive intelligence. He realizes the abnormal within his known environment. He does not react the same way in strange environments since he does not know what is normal.

On the more serious side is a fear of people. This can result in backing off, seeking his own space and saying "leave me alone" or it can result in an aggressive behavior that may lead to challenging the person. Respect that the dog wants to be left alone and give him time to come forward. If you approach the cornered dog, he may resort to snapping. If you leave him alone, he may decide to come forward, which should be rewarded with a treat. Years ago we had a dog that behaved in this manner. We coaxed people to stop by the house and make friends with our fearful dog. She learned to take the treats and after weeks of work she overcame her suspicions and made friends more readily.

Some dogs may initially be too fearful to take treats. In these cases it is helpful to make sure the dog hasn't eaten for about 24 hours. Being a little hungry encourages him to accept the treats, especially if they are of the "gourmet" variety. I have a dog that worries about strangers since people seldom stop by my house. Over the years she has learned a cue and jumps up quickly to visit anyone sitting on the sofa. She learned by herself that all guests on the sofa were to be trusted friends. I think she felt more comfortable with them being at her level, rather than towering over her.

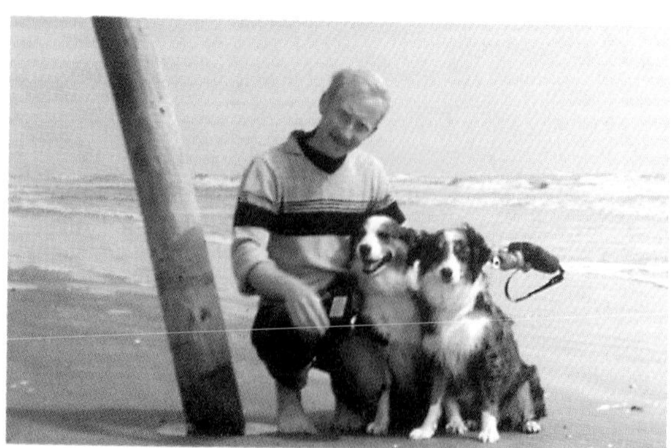

Introducing your Aussie to various places and situations will help him become well socialized in any environment.

Dogs can be afraid of numerous things, including loud noises and thunderstorms. Invariably the owner rewards (by comforting) the dog when it shows signs of fearfulness. I had a terrible problem with my favorite dog in the Utility obedience class. Not only was he intimidated in the class but he was afraid of noise and afraid of displeasing me. Frequently he would knock down the bar jump, which clattered dreadfully. I gave him credit because he continued to try to clear it, although he was terribly scared. I finally learned to "reward" him every time he knocked down the jump. I would jump up and down, clap my hands and tell him how great he was. My psychology worked, he relaxed and eventually cleared the jump with ease. When your dog is frightened, direct his attention to something else and act happy. Don't dwell on his fright.

Allow different people to handle and pet your Australian Shepherd. The more friends he makes, the less fearful he will be of strangers.

A fearful Australian Shepherd will not be useful as a herding or working dog. If you plan to work with your Aussie, socialize him with the animals he will be dealing with.

AGGRESSION

Some different types of aggression are: predatory, defensive, dominance, possessive, protective, fear induced, noise provoked, "rage" syndrome (unprovoked aggression), maternal and aggression directed toward other dogs. Aggression is the most common behavioral problem encountered. Protective breeds are expected to be more aggressive than others but with the proper upbringing they can make very dependable companions. You need to be able to read your dog.

The high jump may seem daunting to your Aussie at first, but if you start small, are patient and reward him, he is sure to be clearing the height in no time.

Many factors contribute to aggression including genetics and environment. An improper environment, which may include the living conditions, lack of social life, excessive punishment, being attacked or frightened by an aggressive dog, etc., can all influence a dog's behavior. Even spoiling him and giving too much praise may be detrimental. Isolation and the lack of human contact or exposure to frequent teasing by children or adults also can ruin a good dog.

Lack of direction, fear, or confusion lead to aggression in those dogs that are so inclined. Any obedience exercise, even the sit and down, can direct the dog and overcome fear and/or confusion. Every dog should learn these commands as a youngster, and there should be periodic reinforcement.

When a dog is showing signs of aggression, you should speak calmly (no screaming or hysterics) and firmly give a command that he understands, such as the sit. As soon as your dog obeys, you have assumed your dominant position. Aggression presents a problem because there may be danger to others. Sometimes it is an emotional issue. Owners may consciously or unconsciously encourage their dog's aggression. Other owners show responsibility by accepting the problem and taking measures to keep it under control. The owner is responsible for his dog's actions, and it is not wise to take a chance on someone being bitten, especially a child. Euthanasia is the solution for some owners and in severe cases this may be the best choice. However, few dogs are that dangerous and very few are that much of a threat to their owners. If caution is exercised and professional help is gained early on, then I

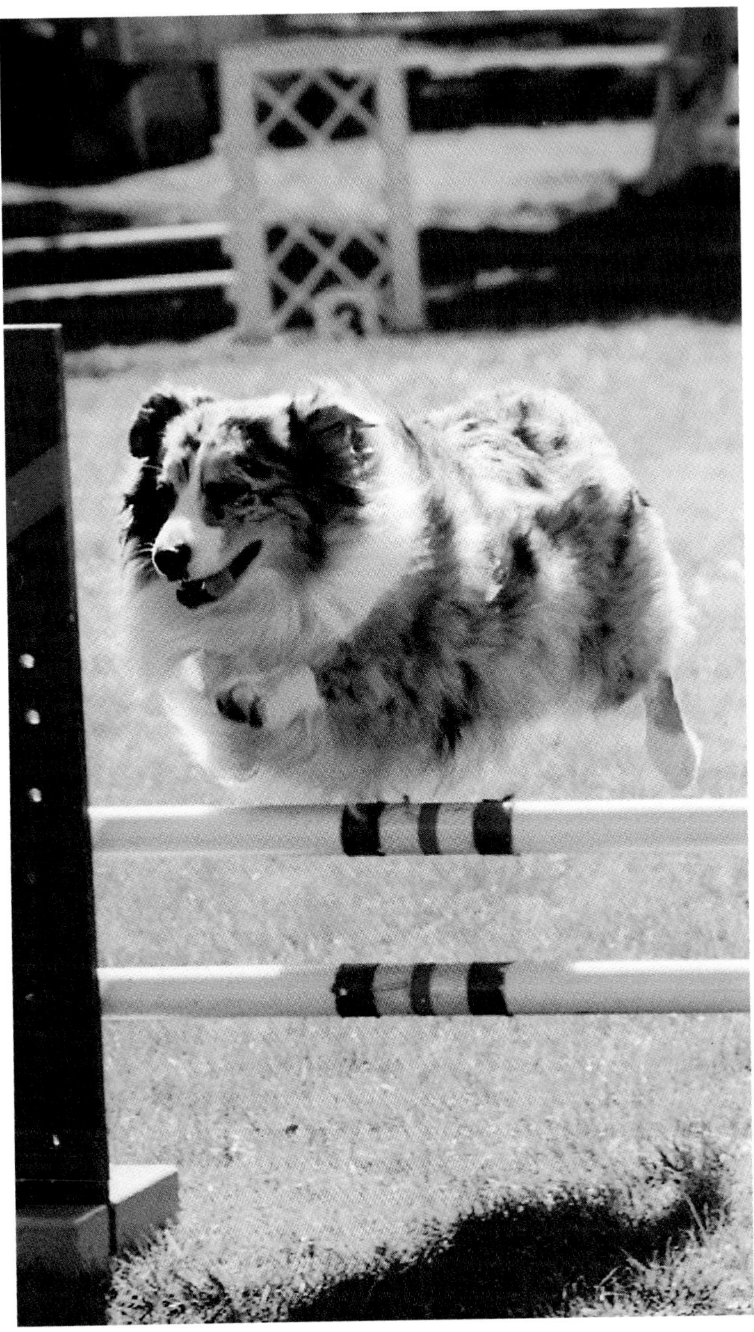

surmise most cases can be controlled.

Some authorities recommend feeding a lower protein (less than 20 percent) diet. They believe this can aid in reducing aggression. If the dog loses weight, then vegetable oil can be added. Veterinarians and behaviorists are having some success with pharmacology. In many cases treatment is possible and can improve the situation.

If you have done everything according to "the book" regarding training and socializing and are still having a behavior problem, don't procrastinate. It is important that the problem gets attention before it is out of hand. It is estimated that 20 percent of a veterinarian's time may be devoted to dealing with problems before they become so intolerable that the dog is separated from its home and owner. If your veterinarian isn't able to help, he should refer you to a behaviorist.

PROBLEMS

Barking

This is a habit that shouldn't be encouraged. Over the years I've had new puppy owners call to say that their dog hasn't learned to bark. I assure them they are indeed fortunate but not to worry. Some owners desire their dog to bark so as to be a watchdog. In my experience, most dogs will bark when a stranger comes to the door.

The new puppy frequently barks or whines in the crate in his strange environment and the owner reinforces the puppy's bad behavior by going to him during the night. This is a no-no. I tell my new owners to smack the top of the crate and say "quiet" in a loud, firm voice. The puppies don't like to hear the loud noise of the crate being banged. If the barking is sleep-interrupting, then the owner should take crate and pup to the bedroom for a few days until the puppy becomes adjusted to his new environment. Otherwise ignore the barking during the night.

Barking can be an inherited problem or a bad habit learned through the environment. It takes dedication to stop the barking. Attention should be paid to the cause of the barking. Does the dog seek attention, does he need to go out, is it feeding time, is it occurring when he is left alone, is it a protective bark, etc.? Presently I have a ten-week-old puppy that is a real loud mouth, which I am sure is an inherited tendency. Both her mother and especially her grandmother are overzealous barkers but fortunately have mellowed with the years. My young puppy is corrected with a firm "no" and gentle shaking and she is responding. When barking presents a problem for you, try to stop it as soon as it begins.

There are electronic collars available that are supposed to curb barking. Personally I have not had experience with them. There are some disadvantages to to the collar. If the dog is barking out of excitement, punishment is not the appropriate treatment. Presumably there is the chance the collar could be activated by other stimuli and thereby punish the dog when it is not barking. Should you decide to use one, then you should seek help from a person with experience with that type of collar. In my opinion I feel the root of the problem needs to be investigated and corrected.

Do not let your Aussie eat from the table. This is a bad habit that will be hard to break.

In extreme circumstances (usually when there is a problem with the neighbors), some people have resorted to having their dogs debarked. I caution you that the dog continues to bark but usually only a squeaking sound is heard. Frequently the vocal cords grow back. Probably the biggest concern is that the dog can be left with scar tissue which can narrow the opening to the trachea.

Jumping Up

Personally, I am not thrilled when other dogs jump on me but I have hurt feelings if they don't! I do encourage my own dogs to jump on me, on command. Some do and some don't. In my opinion, a dog that jumps up is a happy dog. Nevertheless few guests appreciate dogs jumping on them. Clothes get footprinted and/or snagged.

I am a believer in allowing the puppy to jump up during his first few weeks. In my opinion if you correct him too soon and at the wrong age you may intimidate him. Consequently he could be timid around humans later in his life. However, there will come a time, probably around four months of age, that he needs to know when it is okay to jump and when he is to show off good manners by sitting instead.

Some authorities never allow jumping. If you are irritated by your dog jumping up on you, then you should discourage it from the beginning. A larger breed of dog can cause harm to a senior citizen. Some are quite fragile. It may not take much to cause a topple that could break a hip.

How do you correct the problem? All family members need to participate in teaching the puppy to sit as soon as he starts to jump up. The sit must be practiced every time he starts to jump up. Don't forget to praise him for his good behavior. If an older dog has acquired the habit, grasp his paws and squeeze tightly. Give a firm "No." He'll soon catch on. Remember the entire family must take part. Each time you allow him to jump up you go back a step in training.

Biting

All puppies bite and try to chew on your fingers, toes, arms, etc. This is the time to teach them to be gentle and not bite hard. Put your fingers in your puppy's mouth and if he bites too hard then say "easy" and let him know he's hurting you. I squeal and act like I have been seriously hurt. If the puppy plays too rough and doesn't respond to your corrections, then he needs "Time Out" in his crate. You should be particularly careful with young children and puppies who still have their

Some dogs may exhibit behavior problems, such as barking. Stop this behavior as soon as it manifests itself in order to avoid problems later.

deciduous (baby) teeth. Those teeth are like needles and can leave little scars on youngsters. My adult daughter still has a small scar on her face from when she teased an eight-week-old puppy as an eight-year-old.

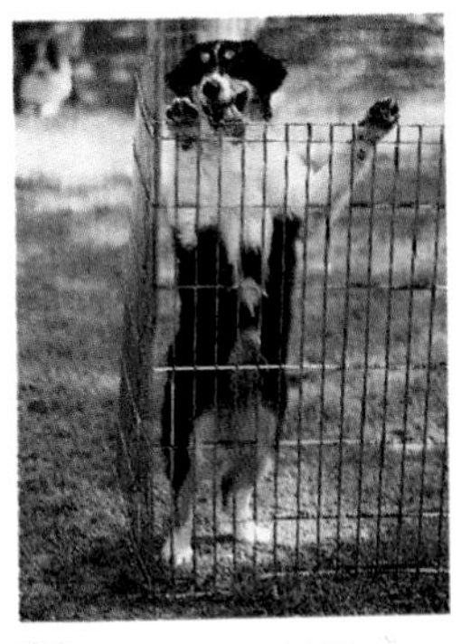
Discourage your Aussie from jumping up on people. He may do it as a sign of affection, but most people do not appreciate paw prints on their clothes.

Biting in the more mature dog is something that should be prevented at all costs. Should it occur I would quickly let him know in no uncertain terms that biting will not be tolerated. When biting is directed toward another dog (dog fight), don't get in the middle of it. On more than one occasion I have had to separate a couple of my dogs and usually was in the middle of that one last lunge by the offender. Some authorities recommend breaking up a fight by elevating the hind legs. This would only be possible if there was a person for each dog. Obviously it would be hard to fight with the hind legs off the ground. A dog bite is serious and should be given attention. Wash the bite with soap and water and contact your doctor. It is important to know the status of the offender's rabies vaccination.

I have several dogs that are sensitive to having mats combed out of their coats and eventually they have had enough. They give fair warning by turning and acting like they would like to nip my offending fingers. However, one verbal warning from me says, "I'm sorry, don't you dare think about biting me and please let me carefully comb just a little bit more." I have owned a minimum of 30 dogs and raised many more puppies and have yet to have one of my dogs bite me except during that last lunge in the two or three dog fights I felt compelled to break up. My dogs wouldn't dare bite me. They know who is boss.

This is not always the case for other owners. I do not wish to frighten you but when biting occurs you should seek professional help at once. On the other hand you must not let your dog intimidate you and be so afraid of a bite that you can't discipline him. Professional help through your veterinarian, dog trainer and/or behaviorist can give you guidance.

Digging

Bored dogs release their frustrations through mischievous behavior such as digging. For the life of me I do not understand why people own dogs only to keep them outside. Dogs shouldn't be left unattended outside, even if they are in a fenced-in yard. Usually the dog is sent to "jail" (the backyard) because the owner can't tolerate him in the house. The culprit feels socially deprived and needs to be included in the owner's life. The owner has neglected the dog's training. The dog has not developed into the companion we desire. If you are one of these owners, then perhaps it is possible for you to change. Give him another chance. Some owners object to their dog's unkempt coat and doggy odor. See that he is groomed on a regular schedule and look into some training classes.

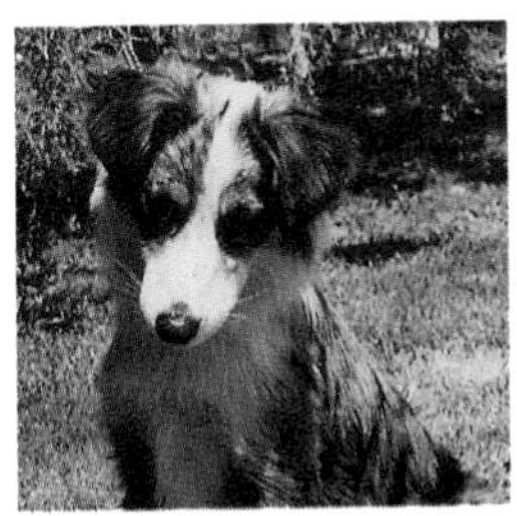

Good temperament is passed from parents to offspring. Your Aussie breeder should carefully screen his dogs in order to produce the best possible puppies.

Submissive Urination

This is not a housebreaking problem. It can occur in all breeds and may be more prevalent in some breeds. Usually it occurs in puppies but occasionally it occurs in older dogs and may be in response to physical praise. Try verbal praise or ignoring your dog until after he has had a chance to relieve himself. Scolding will only make the problem worse. Many dogs outgrow this problem.

Coprophagia

Also known as stool eating, sometimes occurs without a cause. It may begin with boredom and then becomes a habit that is hard to break. Your best remedy is to keep the puppy on a leash and keep the yard picked up. Then he won't have an opportunity to get in trouble. I do not like to clean up accidents or "poop scoop" the yard in front of puppies. I'm suspicious that

Children make great playmates for your Australian Shepherd. Most of all, caring for a dog teaches children responsibility and respect for animals.

some puppies try to help and will clean up the stool before I have a chance. Your veterinarian can dispense a medication that is put on the dog's food that makes the stool taste bitter. Of course this will do little good if your dog cleans up after other dogs.

The Runaway

There is little excuse for a dog to run away since dogs should never be off leash except when supervised in the fenced-in yard.

I receive phone calls on a regular basis from prospective owners that want to purchase a female since a male is inclined to roam. It is true that an intact male is inclined to roam, which is one of the reasons a male should be neutered. However, females will roam also, especially if they are in heat. Regardless, these dogs should never be given this opportunity. A few years ago one of our clients elected euthanasia for her elderly dog that radiographically appeared to

An Australian Shepherd on his back, belly exposed, submits to his owner's dominant role - and gets an enjoyable tummy rub.

have an intestinal blockage. The veterinarian suggested it might be a corncob. She assured him that was not possible since they hadn't had any. Apparently he roamed and raided the neighbor's garbage and you guessed it–he had a corncob blocking his intestines. Another dog raided the neighbor's garbage and died from toxins from the garbage.

To give the benefit of the doubt, perhaps your dog escapes or perhaps you are playing with your dog in the yard and he refuses to come when called. You now have a runaway. I have had this happen on a smaller scale in the house and have, even to my embarrassment, witnessed this in the obedience ring. Help! The first thing to remember is when you finally do catch your naughty dog, you must not discipline him. The reasoning behind this is that it is quite possible there could be a repeat performance, and it would be nice if the next time he would respond to your sweet command.

Always take your dog out on a lead to prevent him from running away or getting lost. This way your Aussie never gets the chance to take off unsupervised.

Always kneel down when trying to catch the runaway. Dogs are afraid of people standing over them. Also it would be helpful to have a treat or a favorite toy to help entice him to your side. After that initial runaway experience, start practicing the recall with your dog. You can let him drag a long line (clothesline) and randomly call him and then reel him in. Let him touch you first. Reaching for the dog can frighten him. Each time he comes you reward him with a treat and eventually he should get the idea that this is a nice experience. The long line prevents him from really getting out of hand. My dogs tend to come promptly within about 3 to 4 feet (out of reach) and then turn tail and run. It's "catch me if you can." At least with the long line you can step on it and stop him.

Food Guarding

If you see signs of your puppy guarding his food, then you should take immediate steps to correct the problem. It is not fair to your puppy to feed him in a busy environment where children or other pets may interfere with his eating. This can be the cause of food guarding. I always recommend that my puppies be fed in their crates where they do not feel threatened. Another advantage of this is that the puppy gets down to the business of eating and doesn't fool around. Perhaps you have seen possessiveness over the food bowl or his toys. Start by feeding him out of your hand and teach him that it is okay for you to remove his food bowl or toy and that you most assuredly will return it to him. If your dog is truly a bad actor and intimidates you, try keeping him on leash and perhaps sit next to him making happy talk. At feeding time make him work for his reward (his dinner) by doing some obedience command such as sit or down. Before your problem gets out of control you should get professional help. If he is out of control over toys, perhaps you should dispose of them or at least put them away when young children are around.

Too many puppies fighting over dinner can lead to food guarding. Feed each dog individually in a calm environment to allow him to make the most of his meal.

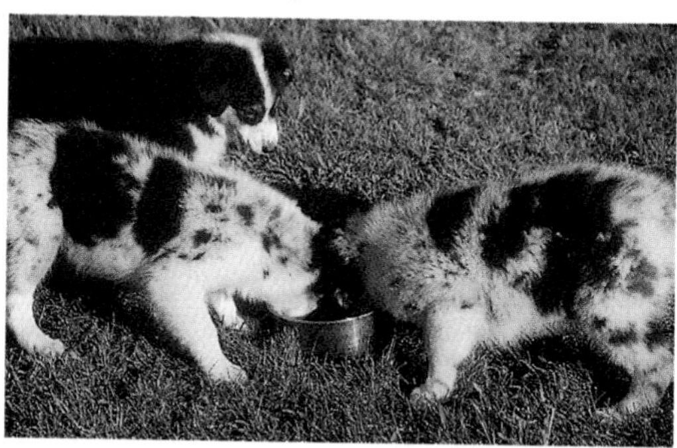

Mischief and Misbehavior

All puppies and even some adult dogs will get into mischief at some time in their lives. You should start by "puppy proofing" your house. Even so it is impossible to have a sterile environment. For instance, if you would be down to four walls and a floor your dog could still chew a hole in the wall. What do you do? Remember puppies should never be left unsupervised so let us go on to the trusted adult dog that has misbehaved. His behavior may be an attention getter. Dogs, and even children, are known to do mischief even though they know they will be punished. Your puppy/dog will benefit from more attention and new direction. He may benefit from a

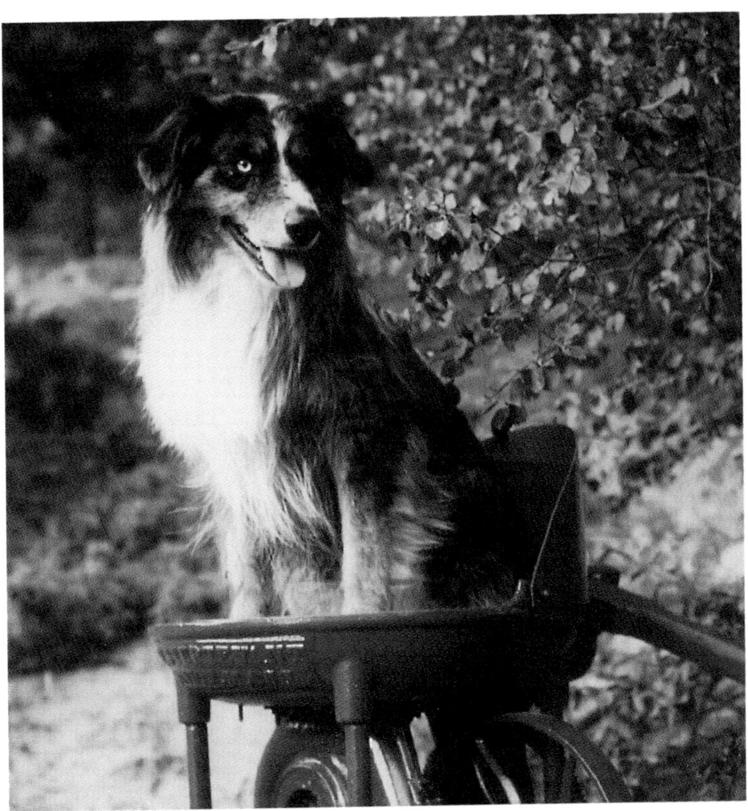

Does this look like the face of a mischief maker? Always keep a close eye on your dog and keep him out of trouble.

training class or by reinforcing the obedience he has already learned. How about a daily walk? That could be a good outlet for your dog, time together and exercise for both of you.

Separation Anxiety

This occurs when dogs feel distress or apprehension when separated from their owners. One of the mistakes owners make is to set their dogs up for their departure. Some authorities recommend paying little attention to the pet for at least ten minutes before leaving and for the first ten minutes after you arrive home. The dog isn't cued to the fact you are leaving and if you keep it low-key they learn to accept it as a normal everyday occurrence. Those dogs that are used to being crated usually accept your departure. Dogs that are anxious may have a serious problem and wreak havoc on the house within a few minutes after your departure. You can try to acclimate your dog to the separation by leaving for just a few minutes at a time, returning and rewarding him with a treat. Don't get too carried away. Plan on this process taking a long time. A behaviorist can set down a schedule for you. Those dogs that are insecure, such as ones obtained from a humane shelter or those that have changed homes, present more of a problem.

Punishment

A puppy should learn that correction is sometimes necessary and should not question your authority. An older dog that has never received correction may retaliate. In my opinion there will be a time for physical punishment but this does not mean hitting the dog. Do not use newspapers, fly swatters, etc. One type of correction, that is used by the mother dog when she corrects her puppies, is to take the puppy by the scruff and shake him *gently*. For the older, larger dog you can grab the scruff, one hand on each side of his neck, and lift his legs off the ground. This is effective since dogs feel intimidated when their feet are off the ground. Timing is of the utmost importance when punishment is necessary. Depending on the degree of fault, you might want to reinforce punishment by ignoring your dog for 15 to 20 minutes. Whatever you do, do not overdo corrections or they will lose value.

My most important advice to you is to be aware of your dog's actions. Even so, remember dogs are dogs and will behave as such even though we might like them to be perfect little people. You and your dog will become neurotic if you worry about every little indiscretion. When there is reason for concern–don't waste time. Seek guidance. Dogs are meant to be loved and enjoyed.

References:

Manual of Canine Behavior, Valerie O'Farrell, British Small Animal Veterinary Association.

Good Owners, Great Dogs, Brian Kilcommons, Warner Books.

SUGGESTED READING

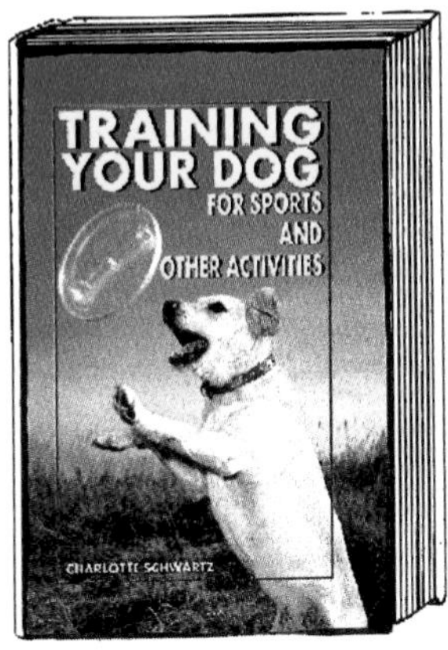

TS-258
Training Your Dog For Sports and Other Activities
160 pages, over 200 full-color photos.

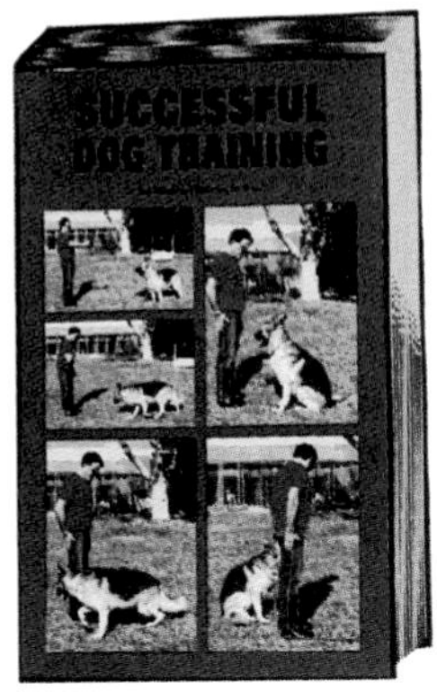

TS-205
Successful Dog Training
160 pages, 130 full-color photos.

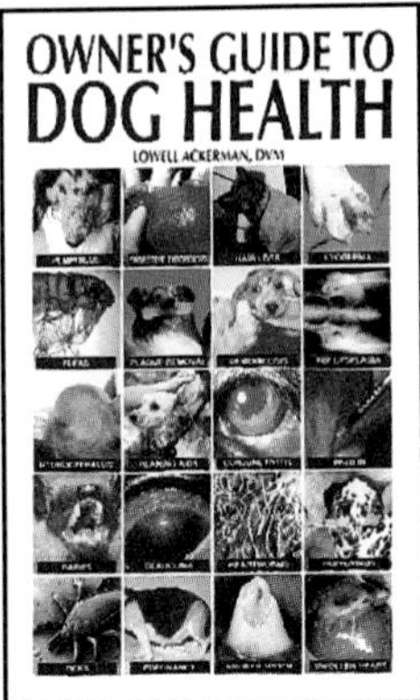

TS- 214
Owner's Guide to Dog Health
432 pages, over 300 full-color photos.

TS-249
Skin and Coat Care For Your Dog
224 pages, over 190 full-color photos.

Index